DAVE CLAYTO

JESUS
NEXT DOOR

A 30-Day Prayer Guide
to Help You Practically Love
the People Around You

CONTENTS

START HERE

When asked to pinpoint what mattered most to God, Jesus did not beat around the bush or speak in code. He said (to paraphrase), "This is what matters most to God: Love the Lord your God with the entirety of who you are and love your neighbors as much as you love yourself" (Matt. 22:37–39). Even though Jesus' words in Matthew 22 are crystal clear, most followers of Jesus will be quick to admit that they struggle to live them out.

I am convinced the journey to becoming a person shaped by the two greatest commandments—to love God and love people— often begins in the place of prayer. God is love and loves all people. I have found that if I consistently come into his presence through prayer, it is impossible to not begin loving God and those around me more fully.

This is the simple focus of this thirty-day prayer journey. It is designed to help you practically grow in love for God and the people he has already put around you in the places where you live, work, and play.

As we get started, here are a few practical suggestions to help you get the most from this prayer journey:

 ## # 1 CHOOSE PEOPLE TO PRAY *FOR*

Since this guide is designed to help you pray for the people God has already put around you, it is important that you begin this journey by identifying a few people for whom you plan to pray each day. You can pray for your next-door neighbors, your co-workers, friends from school, the barista at your favorite coffee shop, or someone in your own family. You get to choose. But before you go any further, take a moment to write down the names of the people for whom you will commit to pray each day over the course of the next month.

Neena   Oscar

Mum   Rose Hoover

JV   Kendall

Megan Montgomery

2 CHOOSE YOUR PEOPLE TO PRAY *WITH*

Once you have determined whom you will pray for, take a minute to identify *who you will pray with* during this season of prayer. Learning to pray not only *for others* but also *with others* will revolutionize your life with Jesus. We are made for community, and, like nearly everything else in life, prayer is better when experienced with other followers of Jesus. Make it a priority to pray together throughout the month, whether in person or through a virtual platform like phone calls, text messaging, or video chats. Get creative, but stay connected to others!

Sami

Michel

Addie

 # 3 ESTABLISH A DAILY ROUTINE

It amazes me how God can use a series of seemingly small but intentional choices to bring about monumental change in our lives. Don't underestimate the power of establishing a daily prayer routine as you begin this journey of praying for and with other people. What follows is a list of simple ideas to help you establish a daily prayer routine:

 Find a Quiet Spot

It doesn't matter if it is a comfortable chair in your home, a park bench along the trail you enjoy walking, or your favorite table at a local coffee shop. Simply find a spot each day where you can give God your undivided attention.

 Clear Your Mind

Jot down any overwhelming thoughts or nagging items that might keep you from enjoying God in prayer on your mental to-do list. Some of these items will be things you might need to discuss with God in prayer, while others will be distractions that you can address later in your day. Take it a step further by turning off your phone to free yourself from unwanted distraction. Finally, set aside two minutes to simply sit in silence with God. Before you ask him for anything, enjoy the gift of his presence.

 Read, Reflect, and Pray

Each daily meditation contains a short devotional thought, a passage of Scripture to read, a few questions for reflection, and daily prayer points to guide you as you pray for yourself and those around you.

Like a spiritual appetizer, this guide is here simply to help get your conversations with God started each day, but my hope is that this will be a springboard into deeper places with God each day.

 ## Take Action

Finally, I believe God will give you ample opportunities each day to actively participate in the ways of Jesus as you pray for those God has placed around you. Jesus says we are blessed when we put his words into practice, so proactively look for opportunities and take a step of faith as God prompts you each day.

JESUS NEXT DOOR

"The word became flesh and made
his dwelling among us."
— John 1:14

SEVERAL MONTHS AGO, our dear friends and neighbors Chris and Lacey delivered the heartbreaking news that they were moving out of our neighborhood to another house just a few miles away. We were so grateful they weren't leaving our city, but we were also sad to hear the news, especially as we began to imagine what the neighborhood would be like without them. Sure enough: Once they moved out, their absence was palpable.

Despite our sadness, it is amazing how God used their *absence to teach me about the importance of presence.*

God used their time in our neighborhood not only to bless our family but also to encourage so many of the people living on our street. We watched first-hand as they built friendships, comforted the hurting, brought people together in life-giving community, and consistently made space to partner with God in the work he was already doing in the lives of people right around them.

To put it simply, God used Chris and Lacey to remind me of Jesus' simple yet crystal-clear call on my life to be a good neighbor as well.

Their absence opened the door for me to reflect on my own life. I wondered,

> If our family moved out of our neighborhood tomorrow, would our neighbors miss us?

Truthfully, my answer differs depending on the day. I would guess that given time to reflect on this question, you might feel similarly about your presence in your neighborhood.

Recently, I found myself wondering what it would be like if I moved out of my house and Jesus moved in: *How would life get better for my neighbors if Jesus were their neighbor? What conversations would he have with them while checking the mail? What needs would he see that I tend to overlook? How would his presence bring transformational joy and life to the people living on my street if he were the one living in my house . . . in my place?*

I love the way John describes this moment in some of the opening words of his account of Jesus' life in the Gospel of John. To paraphrase, he says, "The infinite God has moved into the neighborhood! God himself is living on our street, and we have experienced just how good it is to have him as our neighbor!"

As you begin this month-long journey of prayer, ask God to help you live as though you were the very hands, feet, and voice of

Jesus to your neighbors—and to everyone you encounter on a daily basis.

GOING DEEPER

 Read: John 1:1–18

 Reflect

▶ If you had to rank yourself as a neighbor, what score would you give yourself on a scale from one to ten? Why?
▶ In what ways are you currently living as a good neighbor to those around you?
▶ In what ways could you improve?

 Pray

▶ Father, please help me to live like your Son Jesus everywhere I live, work, and play.
▶ Father, please give me the desire to live as a good neighbor.
▶ Father, please give me new opportunities to share your love with the people around me.
▶ Father, please begin to awaken each of my neighbors to your unending love for them.

Father, Please Help Me

BE A GOOD NEIGHBOR

"And *who is my neighbor*?"

— Luke 10:29

THE GREAT AMERICAN writer Mark Twain supposedly once said, "Some people are troubled by the things in the Bible they can't understand, but the things that trouble me most are the things I can understand." In other words, Twain knew his biggest challenge, when it came to encountering God through the Bible, was not a *lack of understanding* but ultimately a *lack of obedience.*

I have often thought of this quote while reflecting on my own faith journey, and I can't help but see this reality unfolding in the story of the Good Samaritan. An expert in the Old Testament Law had arrived on the scene to challenge Jesus and he knew "the right answers." He was well aware that what mattered most to God was a deep love for God expressed practically through loving our neighbors (see Luke 10:26–28).

This expert in the Law already understood God's will for his life.

> He didn't need a greater level
> of *understanding*; he needed a
> greater level of *obedience*.

As they continued to talk, Jesus expanded the borders of this man's imagination regarding who should be the object of this kind of love. When asked, "Who is my neighbor?" Jesus answered that simple question by telling the now famous story about a traveler who demonstrated great love toward a desperate stranger lying in need on the side of the road.

Jesus told this story to show us that our neighbor isn't just the person living next door to us (although it certainly starts there, as we saw yesterday); it is any person we encounter in our daily path who needs to be touched by the love of God through us.

Like Twain, I usually don't need more understanding when it comes to loving those around me; I need a greater level of joy-filled obedience. Can you imagine what would happen if every follower of Jesus actually lived out this God-glorifying, others-focused kind of love? It would change the world.

A dear friend and mentor of mine would often say, "Pay attention to the people God puts in your path."

I am convinced that each one of us will be given multiple opportunities to love someone well today in the name of Jesus. Your day may be filled with divine appointments; the question is this: Will you notice them? It might be your actual next-door neighbor, or it might be the woman who sits next to you at work. It could be a college student who serves your coffee, a frustrated stranger in the lane next to you on your morning commute, or a roommate who needs your undivided attention.

As you pray today, ask God to help you *live as a good neighbor* toward anyone and everyone he might place in your path.

GOING DEEPER

 Read: Luke 10:25–37

 Reflect

▶ How many people can you name who live in the houses or apartments closest to you?
▶ What are the names of the people at your school or office whom you see on a regular basis?
▶ Can you list specific names of people from the places you frequent (e.g., the coffee shop, gym, or golf course)?

 Pray

▶ Father, please help me to notice the people you have placed in my path.
▶ Father, please help me to see the physical, emotional, and relational needs of the people around me today.
▶ Father, please use me to bless someone's life today in the name of Jesus.
▶ Father, please soften the hearts of those around me.

Father, Please Help Me

LIVE HERE WITH PURPOSE

"He decided exactly when they should live. And he decided exactly where they should live. . . . so that people would seek him. And perhaps they would reach out for him and find him."

— Acts 17:26–27 (NIrV)

RECENTLY, A COUPLE of young women I know began asking God where they should live. To their parents, the answer was simple: somewhere affordable and safe. But to these women, it wasn't that simple. As they prayed, they kept sensing the Holy Spirit nudging them to investigate a part of town that was affordable—but certainly not safe. Their parents were obviously not thrilled with the idea.

After prayer-walking one neighborhood in particular and talking with the people sitting on their front porches in that neighborhood, these ladies found a small place they could afford. Their parents did not want them to drive through this part of town, much less live there. Yet after several hard conversations and much prayer, they received their parents' blessing and moved in.

Soon after, it became clear that God had been preparing the way for them. They immediately found favor with the kids and the kids' families in their new neighborhood. In fact, their house became the place to hang out after school. Afternoon snacks and conversations eventually led to tutoring, Bible studies, and deep relationships. Over the course of time, several of the kids gave their lives to Jesus, and their family members began to trust and follow Jesus as well.

It is amazing what happens when we begin to realize that our homes are not supposed to be an escape from the world around us but actually an outpost of God's kingdom.

Imagine what would happen in your city if every follower of Jesus truly believed their home was designed to display the goodness of Jesus so those who live near them could see it.

Have you ever stopped to reflect on the mystery of how you came to live in the place where you are now living? Sure, maybe you can attribute it to some of your own decisions and perhaps you know why you chose your specific college or neighborhood or city. Maybe you can even pinpoint why you stepped into your current career or accepted that recent job offer.

But think back even further to get a sense of God's work in your life. How did your parents end up in the city in which you were born? What decisions led your grandparents to settle down where they did? What brought your relatives to this country years ago?

Now, let's think even further back.

When I sit in the simple mystery of my existence, it stirs up within me awe and deep hunger for more of God. His ability to orchestrate the details of our lives—not only for his glory but also for our good—is absolutely astounding.

But the words of Acts 17:26–27 (quoted above) go beyond what's good for us and his glory. They come from the apostle Paul's speech to the philosophers in Athens. He reminds us that not only is God able to work for his glory and our good, but he also manages to do so in a way that benefits those who are living right around us.

> Paul declares that God not only chose *when you would live* but also *where you would live*.

He goes on to say that he made these decisions so those living around you would seek God and find him.

Have you ever stopped to ponder how God has perfectly positioned you for the sake of those around you? I wonder how God wants to use your story to help those around you see his work in their lives?

When you look out of your front door today or when you bump into that person in the elevator at work, take a moment to ask God to help you see his plans for placing you where he has placed you. Ask him to help you make the most of every opportunity.

Ask him to help you know how to share the reason for the hope you have in Jesus today.

GOING DEEPER

 Read: Acts 17:16–34

 Reflect

▶ As you reflect on your life, where have you seen God work through you in the places where you live, work, or play?
▶ How did you end up where you currently work or go to school?
▶ Why do you think God has placed you where you are in general?

 Pray

▶ Father, please open my eyes to your purposes for me in the places where you have planted my feet.
▶ Father, help me to live with a great sense of intentionality in all of the places I will find myself today.
▶ Father, please open the minds of those around me to the beauty of your truth.

Father, Please Help Me

EXPERIENCE YOUR LOVE

"And a voice came from heaven: 'You are my Son, *whom I love*; with you I am well pleased.'"

— Mark 1:11

ON APRIL 10, 1912, a Scottish preacher named John Harper, with his six-year-old daughter and his sister, boarded the Titanic to head for America to preach at a church in Chicago, Illinois, pastored by Dwight L. Moody. Four days later, at 11:40 pm while John was doing his nightly devotions, the Titanic hit an iceberg and began to sink.

John wrapped his six-year-old daughter in a blanket, kissed her on the forehead, and placed her, along with his sister, on a lifeboat. He knew he would likely never see them again. Then, John went up and down the deck of the Titanic, pleading with Christians to give up their spots on the lifeboats so that those who were not yet followers of Jesus could survive and have a chance to be saved by Jesus' transforming love.

John Harper stayed on the boat until the very last moment, when he jumped into the icy water. Those who saw him that night told stories of how he swam from person to person in the cold, dark waters of the Northern Atlantic, sharing the gospel with anyone who would listen before the cold set in and they sank to their death.

There is no denying that the love of God was flowing through the veins of John Harper. He was a man overflowing with the love of heaven.

I'm convinced that human beings, on their own accord, cannot will themselves to love strangers like John Harper did that evening. I think it's literally impossible apart from God.

> Before we can extend divine love,
> we must truly receive divine love.

The words quoted above from Mark 1:11 are critical for our understanding of living on mission with Jesus. Before Jesus had preached any sermons, performed any miracles, or pardoned anyone's sin, God the Father tore open the heavens and audibly affirmed his love for his Son Jesus. The Father spoke his love over Jesus from the beginning of his earthly ministry. This love was not based on *what Jesus did* but instead on *who Jesus was*—the cherished Son of God.

We too have a God-given identity. We're not divine, but we are beloved sons and daughters of the King. I began to understand this truth more fully after each of my children were born. I loved each of my children from the moment they took their first breath—not because of their abilities or behaviors but simply because they were mine.

It is amazing to think this is how God feels about each one of us! He loves you with the same love with which he loves Jesus, not because of what you have accomplished but simply because you are his.

His love for you is not based on your gifts, talents, morality, usefulness, or performance. His love for you compelled him to send Love Incarnate to earth for you in Jesus (John 3:16). It was the Father's love for us in the Son that kept Jesus fastened to the cross on our behalf, while we were still rebelling in our sin-soaked choices.

Romans 5:8 declares this truth, that "God demonstrates his own love for us in this: While we were still sinners, Christ died for us."

Our present and future hope is not grounded in *our* love for God but in *his* love for us. Long before we began to love him, he first loved us. It is only through his initiating love for us that we can begin to reciprocate our love toward God and others.

Before we can live like the Scottish preacher John Harper did, we must come face to face with the God of love who changed John Harper in the first place. Then and only then can we begin to love others as Jesus does.

As you enter into another day of prayer on behalf of those around you, ask God to anchor you in the reality of his love.

Read: Ephesians 3:14–21

 Reflect

▶ When have you recently needed God to forgive you?

▶ Can you think of a moment when you were overwhelmed by the reality of God's love for you?

 Pray

▶ Father, as your Word describes in Ephesians 3:14–21, would you help me to grasp how high and wide and long and deep is your love for me?

▶ Father, will you pour out your love into my heart in fresh ways today?

▶ Father, will you help the people in our city to understand the depth of your love for them?

Father, Please Help Me

BE MOTIVATED BY LOVE

"*For God so loved the world* that he gave his one and only Son, that whoever believes in him shall not perish but have eternal life. For God did not send his Son into the world to condemn the world, but to save the world through him."

— John 3:16–17

ONE OF MY heroes in the faith is Piyas Dey, a man most people have never heard of. He's my friend, my brother in the faith, and one of the most servant-hearted people I know. He and his family serve among the poorest of the poor in East India. They have spent the last decade working tirelessly to feed, clothe, house, and disciple hundreds of children who have been left to fend for themselves in the slums. They do not see these kids as their "ministry project"; they see them as their very own children.

In order to serve these kids, Piyas quit a lucrative job and his family left behind a very comfortable life for a ministry that had no salary and no security whatsoever. From an earthly perspective, it was career suicide; but from a heavenly perspective, it was a huge promotion. Piyas knew that security was not found in his salary but ultimately in his obedience to Jesus. He knew the most secure place in the world was smack dab in the middle of God's will.

Several years ago, on one of my visits to India, I asked Piyas what motivated him and his family to take such a risk for these children.

Without hesitating, he walked me across his small office and showed me a picture he had taken more than ten years earlier of a four-year-old boy eating out of a trash can on the side of the street. God used that defining moment captured in a photograph to arrest his attention and redirect the course of his life (and the lives of all those he has blessed through his ministry). That picture has become his daily reminder of why God called him into the life-long adventure of serving those kids.

Still looking at the picture on his wall, he went on to say, "How can I follow Jesus and not care about the condition of this child?"

"What motivates me?" He said, "It's simple: love."

If a picture is worth a thousand words, God has used that photograph to write a novel on Piyas's heart. That photograph reminds him of God's love, and God's love has become Piyas's driving force. He is compelled to be a good neighbor, not out of duty or obligation, but out of love.

One of my favorite moments in the Bible is found in the short conversation between Jesus and a brilliant religious leader named Nicodemus. After discussing the beauty of God's kingdom, Jesus lets Nicodemus in on God's motivation for sending Jesus to earth—love.

In this moment, Jesus peels back the curtain and allows Nicodemus (and us), to see why Jesus left the comfort and security of heaven. He had a mission, but it wasn't a mission of vengeance as if he came to whip humanity back into shape.

> Jesus came because of love.

Let that sink in. The creator of the universe loved you enough to send his Son to earth for you. But not just for you; he came for your neighbors, your coworkers, your classmates, and even that family member who ruins every Thanksgiving dinner.

How valuable is each and every person you meet? They are worth the price of God's one and only Son.

So don't be surprised if God stops you in your tracks today. He might choose to use someone else's situation—like that boy in Piyas's photograph—as your invitation into his mission of love.

Can you imagine what would happen if you began to see each person around you through the lens of heaven's price tag? What would happen if your actions toward others were driven by that kind of love?

As you enter into another day of praying for those around you, ask God to fill your heart with his love for the people he has placed around you.

Read: John 3:1–21

 Reflect

▶ What would change in the way you treat those around you if you truly believed they were God's beloved children?
▶ How does God's love for each person shift the way you respond to people facing difficult situations?
▶ How does God's love for humanity impact the way you deal with "difficult" people?

 Pray

▶ Father, please help me to see the image of God in every person I meet.
▶ Father, please help me to love each person I encounter today like they belong to you, as they do.
▶ Father, please break my heart for what breaks yours.
▶ Father, please help those around me to know how valuable they are to you.

Father, Please Help Me

PRAY WITH BELIEF

"Therefore I tell you, whatever you ask
for in prayer, *believe that you have
received it*, and it will be yours."
— Mark 11:24

ONE OF MY childhood friends comes from a long line of wealthy people. His family not only made lots of money through their own businesses, but they were also sitting on decades of wealth that had been handed down through their family.

In the truest sense, money was never an issue for them. If they needed something, or even just *wanted* something, they simply bought it.

Fortunately for those around them, they were also exceedingly generous and kind.

My friend—the oldest son in the family—never thought twice about asking his parents for anything. He knew that if his request aligned with his parents' values, then the answer would always be yes.

Jesus teaches us to approach our heavenly Father in a similar way. There is a beautiful moment in Mark 11:24 that reminds me of how my friend approached his earthly father. To paraphrase, Jesus says, "If your prayer lines up with your heavenly Father's plans, then you can go ahead and rest assured his answer will be yes."

> Have you ever been around
> someone who consistently prays
> with this kind of confidence?

I think of my friend Paul, who lived for years depending on God to meet his needs day by day. His prayer life was simply contagious. He spoke with God in ways that stirred a deep longing within me to know God more intimately. Then there's my friend Shodankeh. When he prays, you get a sense that heaven is rearranging history because of the confidence with which he approaches our heavenly Father.

Jesus tells us that whenever we pray in agreement with the will of God, our prayer is as good as answered. The question is this:

Do we believe Jesus is telling us the truth when it comes to how God responds to our faith-filled prayers?

If you're like me, it's easy to affirm the truth without actually believing it. I often allow my personal experiences and disappointments to carry more weight in my life than God's Word. If you struggle to believe Jesus' word about prayer from Mark 11:24, I encourage you to humbly come to God today, like the man in Mark 9:24, who says to Jesus, "I do believe; help me overcome my unbelief!"

How is God inviting you to trust him today? If you had no fear of being disappointed, what would you ask God for today? Is there anyone for whom you have quit praying because you lost faith that Jesus can redeem their life?

As you step into another day of praying, ask God to fill your heart with confidence and boldness as you enter into conversation with him on behalf of your neighbors, coworkers, family members, and friends.

GOING DEEPER

 Read: Mark 11:22–25

 Reflect

▶ Do you have confidence that God hears and answers your prayers?
▶ Can you remember a time when God answered a prayer in such a way that built your trust in his attentiveness and goodness toward you?
▶ Have you allowed any past disappointments to impact the way you approach God in the present? How can you revisit those disappointments in a meaningful way?

Pray

- ▸ Father, please help me to believe Jesus' words when it comes to praying bold, kingdom-centered prayers.
- ▸ Father, please help me to understand your will for my life.
- ▸ Father, please help me to pray by the power of the Holy Spirit in accordance with your will.
- ▸ Father, please bring every single person in my city into a life-changing relationship with Jesus Christ.

DAY 7

Father, Please Help Me

LOVE WITH ACTION

"*I have compassion for these people*;
they have already been with me for
three days and have nothing to eat."
— Mark 8:2

MY FRIENDS MARY and Drew are two of the most compassionate and courageous people I know. Through a series of divinely orchestrated events, God began to open their eyes and hearts to the overwhelming reality of human trafficking that is plaguing certain parts of our city (Nashville, Tennessee). As followers of Jesus, they were convicted that this darkness was not something they could ignore.

They didn't know what to do, but they knew they had to do something.

So with very little in the way of resources or manpower, they simply started showing up for duty, trusting that God would guide their steps.

In the years since, they have stood in awe as God has begun to push back the darkness in amazing ways by redeeming the lives of both the oppressed and the oppressors.

One of the defining characteristics of Jesus, as well as my friends Mary and Drew, is heavenly compassion. People often think of compassion as an overwhelming sympathy toward the needs or suffering of other people. But Jesus' brand of compassion is more than merely feeling sorry for someone; it is feeling so moved by their situation that *you actually help them.*

I love the scene that unfolds in Mark 8, when Jesus finds himself surrounded by thousands of people who had been so hungry to hear him teach that they had ignored their hunger for food—for three days. In the midst of the enormous crowd, Jesus helps his disciples see how he felt about the people. He says, "I have compassion for these people; they . . . have nothing to eat" (Mark 8:2).

If you remember the story, Jesus' friends respond in logical fashion. They essentially say, *Jesus, our supply is not enough to meet their demand.* They had no fast-food restaurants around, and even if they had those around, they didn't have enough money to feed the overwhelming crowd of people. It's easy to be critical of their response since we know how the story ends. But when you put yourself in their shoes, their response seems quite normal.

Have you ever been in a similar position, when your limited resources—physical, relational, emotional, or spiritual—were not sufficient to meet the needs before you? These moments can be overwhelming, and these issues can feel impossible to solve. But in the presence of Jesus they are pregnant with miraculous possibilities.

Before a miracle occurs, there is always a situation that requires a miracle first. If we are honest, we all want to experience a miracle, but we don't want to be in a situation that requires one.

Once the disciples entrusted Jesus with the limitations of their reality, Jesus provided in ways they had never imagined. Not only did he meet their immediate need, but they even had leftovers!

That is the God we serve. He allows us to experience our limitations so we can embrace his breathtaking sufficiency to meet our every need, as well as the needs of those around us. He specializes in defying the odds. He is the Impossibility Specialist. Whenever God is part of the equation, no circumstance is too challenging.

What are you facing that requires a miraculous touch from God? Where do you need Jesus to multiply something in your life to meet the needs of those around you?

> Jesus never asks us to trust him with what we do not have; he simply invites us to trust him with what's in our hands—no matter how big or how small.

I believe Jesus does his best work in and through us when we're in the place of humble dependence on him. I wonder: What would happen if Jesus opened your eyes to the needs of those around you in a new way today? Once he does, don't be surprised if their needs are greater than your capacity to meet them. Remember that the weight of the world's needs rests on

God's shoulders, not on yours. You are merely a conduit of his goodness. Place whatever need you have—big or small—in the hands of Jesus, and sit back in awe as he multiplies the loaves and fish for you and for the good of those around you.

 Read: Mark 8:1–13

 Reflect

▸ Are you able to identify any place of overwhelming need—physical, emotional, relational, or spiritual—in the lives of those around you?
▸ Has God already placed the provision for the needs of those around you in your hands?
▸ Where do you need God to multiply something you have in order to serve someone else?

 Pray

▸ Father, please help me to see how I have already been entrusted to bless others.
▸ Father, please use all you have given me to bless those around me.
▸ Father, please help me to trust you enough to release what's in my hands for the sake of loving others.
▸ Father, please provide for those around me in such a way that they know you see them and love them.

Father, Please Help Me

SERVE OTHERS IN HUMILITY

"Now that I, your Lord and Teacher, have washed your feet, *you also should wash one another's feet.*"

— John 13:14

A FEW YEARS ago, our family had the privilege of living across the street from a remarkable woman who was in her early sixties at the time. Although the first few decades of her life were filled with great pain and struggle, she persevered in a remarkable way. By the time our stories crossed paths, she was a devout follower of Jesus, an excited grandmother, and one of the most creative neighborhood missionaries I have ever been around.

Over the course of her more than fifty years of living in that particular neighborhood, she became overwhelmed by the devastating cycle in which so many young girls would find themselves. So she asked God to give her wisdom on how to help these young, often overlooked, girls break free from the seemingly endless cycle.

Although God has used her in countless ways, it was her continual posture of humble service that gave me a fresh picture of what it might look like if Jesus literally moved into my neighborhood.

Day after day, our family watched as she gave of her time, energy, wisdom, and money to help these young girls get their lives back on track after they had been sidelined by poor choices.

> She didn't get paid for it.
> She rarely got thanked for it.
> But she knew she had been made to do it.

One of my favorite stories from the life of Jesus is recorded in John 13. The story takes place on the eve of Jesus' crucifixion, as he ate one last meal with his closest friends before he went to the cross. In the context of this meal Jesus does something that surprises everyone in the room: He washes his disciples' feet.

John 13:3 tells us that it was Jesus' certainty about where he had come from (his identity) and his certainty about where he was going (his destiny) that gave him the security to humbly serve his friends in such an unimaginable way. In a moment when any normal person would have been concerned with their own well-being—Jesus' actions remind us that he is no ordinary person.

The creator of the universe stooped down to gently wash the very feet of those who would abandon him in their selfishness and fear just a few hours later. Isn't Jesus amazing!?

We can gain courage to follow the humble ways of Jesus in the present only when our past (our identity) and our future (our destiny) have been firmly settled in Jesus.

Jesus was able to take the lowly path because he knew that in due time his heavenly Father would lift him up.

The neighbor I mentioned above served countless young girls, even though she knew she would receive little recognition or thanks. She was able to do this because she too knew that she would hear her heavenly Father say one day, "Well done, good and faithful servant."

What about you? Do you know who you are? Even more important, do you know whose you are? Do you have confidence about your eternal standing with God?

If you do, then I want to encourage you to have the courage to take a step down and go low. Take the path of humility. Whom is Jesus inviting you to serve? Is there someone in your neighborhood, workplace, school, or extended family that needs to experience the love of Jesus through you as you humble yourself to serve them?

As you pray for those around you today, ask God to strengthen your understanding of both your identity and your destiny so that you can follow Jesus in the way of humility.

Read: John 13:1–17

 Reflect

- ▶ Have you ever experienced the love of Jesus through a person who humbly and consistently served you? If so, who?
- ▶ Whom is God inviting you to humbly serve in this season of life?
- ▶ What barriers (if any) in your own life might make it challenging for you to serve others in the name of Jesus?

 Pray

- ▶ Father, please firmly establish my identity in you alone.
- ▶ Father, please help me to love the people around me the way that you love me.
- ▶ Father, please help me to serve the people around me like Jesus has served me.
- ▶ Father, please help the people around me to see what a loving and gracious God you truly are.

Father, Please Help Me

LEARN THEIR NAMES

"'How do you *know me*?' Nathaniel asked."
— John 1:48

BRANDON IS ONE of my closest friends. Not only is he a great friend to me but he is also a beloved pastor to our church family. For more than a decade, Brandon has faithfully served our church and city in a variety of ways—both seen and un-seen. He seems to move effortlessly between teaching God's word, mentoring younger men, and caring for those who are hurting. He is confident and humble, generous and kind. If loving people well were an Olympic sport, Brandon would be a gold medalist.

One evening, after one of our church's Sunday worship gatherings, I found myself in an incredible conversation with a man in his early twenties. In the middle of our conversation, Brandon walked by—at a distance—and this young man stopped me mid-sentence and said, "Man, I love Brandon!"

Due to the nature of our conversation, it caught me by surprise that he would stop the conversation to share what seemed like an inconsequential thought. I was intrigued, so I responded, "That makes me happy. I love him too, but I'm curious: Why do *you* love him?"

I don't know what I expected him to say, but his response caught me by surprise. He said,

> **That's easy—Brandon knows my name.**

Let that sink in for a moment as you think about this simple statement: He knows my name.

I remember moving to Nashville when I was nineteen years old and feeling like a small fish in a big pond. It was one of the first times in my life when I would find myself in a crowded room and yet still feel completely alone. During that season I was always eager to go home to see my family and friends because home was the place where people knew my name. Part of what makes home feel like home is simply that we are known.

I'm convinced that a healthy desire to be known is one of the deepest longings of the human heart.

Can you imagine what it felt like for Nathaniel the day he realized Jesus knew his name? Nathaniel responded, "How do you know me?" In other words, I'm a nobody from a small town, and you have no business paying attention to someone like me. This is similar to what Zacchaeus must have felt when Jesus spotted him in the midst of a huge crowd and called him by name.

One of the hallmarks of Jesus' ministry is that crowds were never just crowds to him. In a sea of seemingly anonymous faces, Jesus saw people created in his image, individuals he knew and loved. The words of John 10:3—that he "calls his own sheep by name and leads them out"—remind us that Jesus is in the business of calling us by name. In fact, I'm convinced that one of the most significant moments in our existence will be the moment we each stand in the presence of the almighty God in the future kingdom of heaven and hear him call us by name.

> It might feel like a small gesture, but taking the time to learn a person's name can leave an eternal impression.

What would it be like if you took the time to learn the names of those you encounter on a regular basis? I wonder how it would impact your coworkers, passers-by at the gym, and the baristas at your favorite coffee spot? I believe, whether they know it right away or not, it will make a lasting impact on them.

Some of the people around you have never had anyone pray for them by name. Perhaps those around you have no family members or friends who are followers of Jesus. What a privilege to bring the names of each person around you before the throne of heaven, into the presence of the One who knows each of us by name.

Read: John 10:10–30

 Reflect

- What does it feel like to be known by those who care about you?
- When have you felt the pain of being unknown or unseen?
- Do you know the names of the people around you? If not, what's holding you back?
- How can you make more time and space in your daily routine to truly notice the people around you?

 Pray

- Father, thank you for knowing me by name.
- Father, will you please help me to learn on a practical level how to remember the names of the people I meet?
- Father, please help me to slow down enough to get to know those you have placed in my path.
- Father, will you help those around me to know in their hearts that you know them by name and love them?

Father, Please Help Me

BE A PEACEFUL PRESENCE

"A furious squall came up, and the waves broke over the boat, so that it was nearly swamped. *Jesus was in the stern, sleeping on a cushion . . .*"

— Mark 4:37–38

OUR CHURCH OFFICE sits on the corner of an increasingly busy intersection. I don't know why, but there seems to be a higher-than-normal rate of high-impact car wrecks just outside of our office windows.

One afternoon, shortly after walking across this intersection toward our office, I saw a large pickup truck come barreling through the intersection before it crashed into the driver's side of a much smaller car. People quickly got out of their cars and rushed to the scene of the accident to make sure everyone was alright. Everyone involved seemed okay, but they were obviously very rattled.

The driver of the smaller car that had been hit was a young woman who was visibly pregnant and quite understandably shaken. As you can imagine, she was quite concerned about the health of her unborn baby. In the midst of all of the pandemonium, a man I did not know and have not seen since walked up to this woman and began speaking peace-filled words of life, encouragement, and strength both to her and to the deeply concerned onlookers who had stopped to help her.

His peace was contagious. Slowly but surely his presence eroded the fear, worry, and anger that was dominating the scene. By the grace of God, the story had a happy—dare I say miraculous—ending and no one was hurt, including the baby. We saw the following truth in action that day:

> In an anxious moment, a peace-filled person is a gift from God.

That's what happened when Jesus calmed the storm in Mark 4. We can easily read this story from the comfort of a coffee shop or a cozy chair and totally miss the pain, fear, and confusion his disciples must have been feeling in the storm. After all, these guys had left everything to follow Jesus, and now they thought they were about to die on the angry seas.

In the midst of this raging storm, Jesus was sound asleep on a cushion in the back of the boat. But when he woke up and calmed the storm, everything changed.

At first glance, Jesus' power nap in the back of the boat was probably not a comforting reality for the disciples. In fact, the disciples' questioning whether or not he even cared for them is a good indicator of how they initially interpreted the moment.

But I'm convinced that in the moments that followed Jesus calming the storm—that day and in the years to come—the disciples looked back on Jesus' ability to sleep in the middle of the storm and began to see it from a different angle.

I wonder if his lack of worry in that terrifying moment began to dismantle their paralyzing fear in the face of uncertainty and impending death. I believe his peace-filled presence became a place of deep strength for each man on that boat.

Jesus offers you that peace right now as well. It's part of the Good News he came to deliver.

Regardless of where you live, work, and play, chances are good that someone around you is currently in the middle of a storm. Maybe their storm is about to capsize their marriage. Maybe their storm is brewing around the lives of their children. Or maybe the winds of their storm threaten their health. There are people all around you who aren't sure if they are going to make it through the storm they are now facing. I wonder how God might be positioning you as a person of peace in the midst of someone's raging storm.

As you pray, ask God to make you an agent of peace for the sake of someone around you today.

Read: Mark 4:35–41

 Reflect

▶ When have you experienced the peace of God through the presence of another person?
▶ Can you recall a time when you experienced internal peace, even though your external circumstances were scary or uncertain?

 Pray

▶ Father, please help me to notice when I am struggling to trust you in the midst of the storms I am facing and teach me to trust you in those moments.
▶ Father, please anchor my heart in your peace.
▶ Father, please use me as an agent of peace to strengthen someone in the storm they are facing.
▶ Father, please help each of the people around me to experience your peace.

DAY 11

Father, Please Help Me

LIFT JESUS HIGHER

"*He must become greater*; I must become less."

— John 3:30

THE CHURCH I have the joy of serving in Nashville rents out music venues for our weekly worship gatherings. A few years ago, after one of our gatherings, several of the employees of the venue showed up and began assembling a stage for the band who was going to perform the next night.

While they rapidly assembled the stage and sound system, I connected with one of the young workers. As I got to know a little bit of his story, it became clear that, like so many others in our city, he had come here with the hope of making it as a performer, but for various reasons his dream was unrealized and discarded.

As we talked, he made a comment that stuck with me:

> I always thought I would be the one standing on the stage, not the one building it for others to stand on.

It was a powerful moment for me.

Living in a city like Nashville, it seems like everyone I meet is an aspiring star. Nearly everyone in our city wants to stand center stage, with or without music. This longing to be front and center is a powerful undercurrent in the human heart, and it impacts all of us—whether we aspire to be a musician, an accountant, a student, a doctor, a stay-at-home parent, or anything else for that matter.

Jesus, however, calls us to take a different path.

At some point in life, every follower of Jesus must to come face-to-face with the reality that this young man was experiencing. We must choose to embrace the reality that life was never intended to revolve around us. Even if our current role in life has us standing at the front of a stage—or in front of a boardroom—we must embrace a purpose far greater than our personal successes.

No matter what you do for a living, you exist to lift Jesus higher.

I love the moment in John 3 when John the Baptist lets us in on his joy. He knew his purpose was to make much of Jesus, he knew he was not the star, and he knew his calling was to set the stage for Jesus, not to stand on it. At a heart level, he believed that the mark of greatness was found not in how many followers he had, how many zeros were on the end of his paycheck, or how great a reputation he had among the crowds. He knew his God-given role on planet earth was to do one thing and one thing alone: to make it easy for people to trust and follow Jesus.

Whether or not you realize it, you too have been put on earth to lift Jesus higher for the sake of those around you. Your life won't look exactly like John the Baptist's—and it shouldn't—but your life can serve a similar purpose. Ask your heavenly Father to use your life to lift Jesus higher today.

GOING DEEPER

 Read: John 3:22–33

 Reflect

▶ Who has God used to help you see Jesus more clearly?
▶ What was it about that person that made Jesus more visible to you?
▶ How are you still living as though life is ultimately about you?

 Pray

▶ Father, please reveal any places in my life where I am still competing with you for getting the glory.
▶ Father, please use my life to make Jesus more visible to those around me.
▶ Father, please give me the heart of John the Baptist, who genuinely longed to see Jesus lifted high.
▶ Father, please free each person around me from any sin that enslaves them.

Father, Please Help Me

GO THE EXTRA MILE

"If anyone forces you to go one
mile, *go with them two miles*."
— Matthew 5:41

FOR MOST OF our marriage, Sydney and I have driven older cars with high mileage. As you might expect with cars like that, we have also had a history of car problems. On a road trip to the lake, just a few months after we married, our car broke down at a rest stop about ninety miles outside of Nashville. Luckily, we were traveling with another car of friends, so we left our car at the rest stop and hopped in their car as we continued to our destination.

When we returned to Nashville several days later, I made plans to retrieve my car from the rest stop. I called my good friend Lee and asked in a sarcastic tone if he wanted the "joy and privilege" of driving me ninety miles to help me fix my car—and then follow me the ninety miles back to Nashville.

For whatever reason, he said yes.

Unfortunately, one of the most embarrassing moments of my adult life soon followed: We pulled up to my broken-down car only to discover that I had accidentally left the keys to my car at home in Nashville!

I was humiliated and felt absolutely terrible for wasting Lee's time.

I will never forget Lee's response. He laughed, made fun of me (as all good friends are supposed to do), and then drove me back to Nashville to get my keys, only to start the trip all over again— that same night!

I can't remember how long it took us in total, but I remember getting home in the early morning hours not too long before the sun rose and a new workday began.

Some friends are willing to help you only when it is convenient; then there are friends like Lee. I cannot think of Jesus' words in Matthew 5 (quoted above) without thinking of Lee and the many others who are so eager to go above and beyond to bless my life.

Have you ever noticed how serving others is rarely convenient?

Just think about Jesus' earthly parents: Can you imagine what Mary and Joseph must have felt when they discovered they would serve God by raising his Son Jesus? What a daunting and delightful task! I wonder: What major life dreams or plans did they surrender in order to say yes to God's plans for them? The truth is, we have no idea what Mary and Joseph had planned for their lives, but we can know with a great deal of certainty that raising God's beloved Son had never crossed their minds.

Although serving God far surpassed their wildest dreams, saying yes to God still came at a cost: They were ridiculed by friends and loved ones, misunderstood, and forced to flee their home in the middle of the night to escape an assassination attempt on their young son's life.

Talk about a change of plans! Serving God for these young parents was good, but it was not convenient.

When it comes to going the extra mile, it is easy for us to be so focused on the price tag that we miss the prize. Did Joseph and Mary have to give up a lot to serve God as they raised his Son? Absolutely. But they also got a front row seat to the life of Jesus! What a privilege. While their obedience certainly came with great cost, it also opened the door for unprecedented experiences and levels of intimacy with God that literally no one else has experienced in quite the same way.

I believe God has great plans for your life, but the reality is that his plans rarely feel *convenient*. His dreams typically don't align with our plans and calendars as seamlessly as we would like them to. Obedience to Jesus often comes with inconvenience.

And yet there is great joy to be found as we go the extra mile!

Just beyond the border of your comfort zone lies a level of intimacy with God only accessible to those willing to say yes to God when it feels—and often is—inconvenient. May we be like Mary who, in the midst of God's surprising and disruptive invitation to her God-given task, responded by saying, "I am the Lord's servant . . . may your word to me be fulfilled" (Luke 1:38).

Ask God to give you the courage to love those around you by going the extra mile today, no matter how inconvenient the opportunity might be.

Read: Matthew 5:38–42

 Reflect

- How do you typically respond to opportunities to go the extra mile?
- Do you have enough margin in your schedule to joyfully go above and beyond in service to others? If not, what can you change to make more room for helping others?
- Who is someone you know who would benefit from your going above and beyond their expectations in the name of Jesus?

 Pray

- Father, help me to obey you, even when it is costly and inconvenient.
- Father, help me to go above and beyond what's expected of me as I love and serve others—even if it's inconvenient for me.
- Father, please use my life to display the goodness of Jesus to those around me.
- Father, please help each of the people around me to experience the blessing of your servant-hearted presence.

Father, Please Help Me

EMBRACE GRACE

"God, who is rich in mercy, made
us alive with Christ even when we
were dead in transgressions—it is *by
grace you have been saved.*"
— Ephesians 2:4–5

IT WAS A rainy Saturday afternoon more than a decade ago when a good friend of mine showed up unexpectedly on our back doorstep. Although I couldn't read his mind, the look on his face told me something was seriously wrong. Over the next few hours, he shared a story of secret sin that had been destroying his life from the inside out and was now making its way to the surface.

For all intents and purposes, it seemed like he was on the verge of losing every thing and every person that had ever mattered to him.

His life was a mess.

In the middle of our tear-drenched conversation, he made a comment that has been firmly planted in my memory ever since. He said,

> *I think I believe* God can forgive me, but I'm not convinced he will ever be able to use me again.

Have you been there before? Have you been so overwhelmed by your own shortcomings that you unintentionally placed a limit on Jesus' redemptive power? Have you ever been tempted to believe the cross of Jesus is powerful enough to clean up your past but not powerful enough to renew your future?

I love that our spiritual missteps can become our greatest testimony when we allow Jesus to shine through. It is through our mess, not our perfection, that Jesus' grace is most clearly displayed to those around us.

If you are anything like me, I am often grateful for God's grace—I just wish I didn't need it.

I love the way Matthew opens his account of Jesus' life. He begins the most important story ever recorded by listing a bunch of seemingly unimportant names. Although Matthew was certainly tracing Jesus' birth to the prophetic promises of the Old Testament for his primarily Jewish audience, there seems to be a deeper purpose as well. I believe Matthew is reminding us that Jesus not only came *for the mess* of humanity, but just as significantly, he came *through the mess*.

Every person in Jesus' family tree desperately needed the grace and mercy Jesus came to offer. Think about some of the stories:

Abraham and Sarah struggled to believe God's promises and, therefore, took things into their own hands, making a mess for the generations to come.

Jacob was a master manipulator, thief, and liar.

Judah took part in enough family problems to be featured on a modern-day reality show.

Rahab slept with men for money.

Jesus' biological family tree was a spiritual mess. If God entered the mess through his very own Son, is it possible he wants to do so in your life—and in the lives of those around you as well?

Jesus came not only *for you*; he also longs to come *through you*. He wants to enter into the messy places of your life. He wants to bring healing and redemption. And he wants to use your life as evidence of his power and kindness to those around you.

In the mess of our lives, Jesus invites us to embrace our need for his grace.

My friend has come a long way since our conversation that rainy Saturday afternoon. God not only forgave his past but he also gave him a new future. The mess that once threatened everything became a beautiful canvas upon which the story of God's transforming power is being displayed for countless others to see.

I wonder how God wants to use your story of redemption today to show those around you the power of his transforming love.

As you enter into another day of prayer, ask God to help you re-call tangible ways you have experienced his grace in your life.

 Read: Ephesians 2:1–10

 Reflect

▶ What parts of your spiritual journey do you prefer to keep hidden from others?
▶ How have you seen God work to redeem the messiest parts of your life?
▶ Is there anyone in your life who could benefit from hearing about how God has transformed your brokenness into something beautiful?

 Pray

▶ Father, please show me the areas of my life that are still a mess.
▶ Father, please help me to trust you with the parts of my life that I often try to hide from you and from others.
▶ Father, please forgive me, heal me, and redeem me.
▶ Father, please use my life as a trophy of your grace so that others around me may see the real Jesus through me.
▶ Father, please help each person I encounter today to turn away from any choices that are keeping them from experiencing intimacy with Jesus.

DAY 14

Father, Please Help Me

SHARE MY STORY

"But *you will receive power* when the Holy
Spirit comes on you; *and you will be my
witnesses* in Jerusalem, and in all Judea and
Samaria, and to the ends of the earth."

— Acts 1:8

EARLIER THIS SUMMER, my lawnmower quit working, so my wife hopped online and found a guy who specializes in repairing small-engine push mowers. A few days later, I loaded up our mower and drove twenty miles south of town to meet him at his mobile repair shop. In less than half an hour, he had not only fixed the problem with my lawnmower but also had sharpened the blade and made my mower cleaner than it had been in years.

Right before he returned my mower, he stopped and said, "Before I can give your mower back, I need to tell you my story."

He went on to briefly, yet powerfully, tell me about the ways Jesus had changed his life: He told me the story of being a closeted alcoholic and a womanizer in college. He described the day he had come to the end of his wits just before God sent a preacher to knock on his door to share the gospel with him. He told me how he was saved by Jesus, went on to marry that preacher's daughter, and pastored two churches. Finally, he shared the joy of being a part-time mechanic but a full-time grandparent. He was overflowing with life.

As he neared the end of his story, he looked me square in the eyes and said,

> " I no longer have a pulpit to preach from, but I still have a story to tell. "

It was amazing. This guy had no idea I was a Christian, much less a pastor. He had merely made a commitment to Jesus that he would take every opportunity to share his story with anyone who would listen.

Right before Jesus returned to heaven, he made a powerful promise to his disciples: "But you will receive power when the Holy Spirit comes on you" (Acts 1:8).

The promise to receive power to witness to others is true for us as well.

Think about a criminal trial. Typically, two types of people are called to the stand to testify. There are experts: those who did not see the crime but have expertise regarding the scene of the crime, the forensics involved, and other pertinent information.

And then there are eyewitnesses.

Even though eyewitnesses are not experts, their testimony is just as powerful as, if not more so than, the qualified experts. You don't have to have a special degree to be an eyewitness; you simply need to have seen, heard, or experienced something.

Jesus' parting promise to us—through his disciples—was that he would fill us with power so we could effectively share our experiences of Jesus with others.

Whether you realize it or not, in Jesus you have a powerful story to tell.

So what's your story?

Do you trust Jesus to fill you, in real time, with the power to share your story with others? You don't have to have a pulpit and you don't have to be a preacher; all you need are the eyes to see what God's doing in your life, the confidence to believe Jesus is with you and has given you power, and the willingness to step out in obedience to testify about his goodness toward you.

You don't need a microphone or a stage to share the story of what Jesus has done in your life. So don't be nervous! The pressure is off, because your story is ultimately not about you. Ask God to give you a clear opportunity to share your story with someone today.

Read: Acts 1:1–11

 Reflect

▶ Take some time to reflect on your journey with Jesus.
▶ If you had to name some key turning points in your relationship with Jesus, what would they be?
▶ When and how did you come to recognize your need for Jesus' love and leadership in your life?
▶ How is Jesus working to actively grow your relationship with him in your current season of life?

 Pray

▶ Father, please give me an awareness of how you have been at work in my life.
▶ Father, please fill me with power and confidence from the Holy Spirit to share my story with someone today.
▶ Father, please use my story to help someone else understand where you have been at work in theirs.

Father, Please Help Me

WELCOME HEAVEN TO EARTH

"Our Father in heaven, hallowed be your
name, your kingdom come, your will be
done, on earth as it is in heaven."
—Matthew 6:9–10

CERTAIN MOMENTS IN life reveal just how thin the space between heaven and earth truly is. One of these moments occurred as our church gathered to worship, to pray, and to baptize new believers into a life of following Jesus. Although these moments are always special, that evening particularly overflowed with the joy of heaven. One aspect that made it so unique was the diversity of backgrounds on display in those who were baptized that night. As each person went under the water, hundreds of people erupted with joy, worship, singing, and dancing. It was, without a doubt, one of the most joy-filled moments of my life, almost indescribably beautiful.

But that evening also had a backstory.

Several years earlier, during a season of prayer and fasting, two of our beloved friends—Jonathan and Shawna—felt called by God to begin giving of their lives in order to love those whom are often overlooked. They were convinced that since heaven is going to be filled with people from every corner of the earth, churches need to begin reflecting that reality right here and now as well. As a result, their family started opening their hearts and lives to what Jesus might have in store among the many people who have come to Nashville from various nations.

As that season of prayer and fasting concluded, God began answering their prayers by leading them to amazing families who had just moved to our city from all around the world. He also started connecting them with incredible Christians who shared their calling and were already faithfully serving among these beautiful yet often overlooked people. Jesus was clearly opening doors.

There we stood, years later, seeing the fruit of what God had been doing all along.

The truth is, the backstory for that evening goes back much further than our friends or the servant-leaders they met here in our city. The backstory finds its origins in the heart of God. In fact, it goes back to the very prayer that Jesus taught us to pray:

> Our Father in heaven, hallowed be your name, your kingdom come, your will be done, on earth as it is in heaven.

I'm convinced Jesus would never ask us to pray a prayer that God is not passionate to answer with a resounding "yes." Notice several important things in Matthew 6:9–13 that Jesus taught his disciples to embrace in order to connect with God in prayer like he did (see the parallel in Luke 11:2–13):

First, he taught that prayer is relational, not transactional: prayer is a conversation with our Father, the King, who loves us deeply and longs to lead us into the good life. Second, the purpose of prayer is about the elevation of God's glory, not our glory. We pray to increase God's fame, not our own. Third, he taught us that prayer plays an important role in welcoming—even ushering in—the reality of heaven to earth.

You can imagine what welcoming heaven to earth might look like by asking questions like these: What would your neighborhood and your workplace (or your school) look like if heaven invaded every heart, home, and habit represented in the people you see there? What would it look like for every relationship to come under the leadership of Jesus? What would happen if every sickness were obliterated, all mental illness cured, and every addictive behavior eradicated? Can you imagine what it would be like if people treated each other with kindness, told only the truth, lived with a healthy balance of work and rest, and worshipped God in all they did?

What would it look like if heaven invaded our world? Not just the world in general—but your world in particular, which is what Jesus' prayer invites us to lean into.

I wonder how you might see the kingdom of heaven tomorrow because of what you pray today. So approach God with joy and boldness as you prayerfully welcome heaven to earth.

Read: Matthew 6:5–18

 Reflect

▸ What people, places, and things do you most often discuss with God in prayer?

▸ If God said yes to all of your prayers, would the people and places around you begin to look more like heaven? How might your prayers need to change?

▸ What aspect of the Lord's Prayer do you most naturally pray? What aspect takes more thought and intentionality for you?

 Pray

▸ Father, please help me to relate to you today as the good Father and King that you are.

▸ Father, please help me to care about the advancement of your name in every interaction I have today.

▸ Father, please help me to live in such a way that heaven touches earth through my life.

▸ Father, please help every person I pass by today to love you as Father and trust you as King.

Father, Please Help Me

SEE JESUS MORE CLEARLY

"Once more Jesus put his hands on the man's eyes. Then his eyes were opened, his sight was restored, and *he saw everything clearly.*"

— Mark 8:25

NEARLY EIGHT YEARS ago, I became friends with an amazing woman who had come to trust and follow Jesus later in her life. She spent her early years walking the path that is more widely traveled. Somewhere in early adulthood, she began reaping the destructive fruit of the seeds she had sown in her years of rebellion, and she found herself at the end of her rope.

God, in his great mercy, found her when she didn't know where to look. As a result, today she is quick to say that Jesus saved her life. For every seed of destruction sown in her years of rebellion she has since sown one hundred seeds of redemption!

I love hearing her share her story because now, in hindsight, she is able to clearly see all the ways Jesus pursued her over the years. She would be the first to say that she didn't just need one encounter with Jesus—she needed many.

Isn't that true for all of us, though?

I am amazed at how long I have been following Jesus, yet I still struggle at times to see him clearly.

> I don't need *a* revival. I have needed *lots* of revivals.

There is a stunning moment of revival that occurs in Mark 8, as Jesus begins to approach the end of his earthly ministry. At this point in Jesus' ministry, his disciples had seen Jesus repeatedly overcome impossible odds (healing the sick, driving out demons, calming the storm, and feeding the multitudes). Yet despite all of their time spent in his presence, the disciples still could not fathom the fullness of their friend Jesus.

In the story, Jesus' first attempt to heal a blind man seemingly failed, because after the first touch from Jesus, the man's vision was only partially restored. It was only after Jesus touched the man a second time that his sight was made perfect.

In the face of the disciples' limited understanding, Jesus used a blind man to shed light on their spiritual blindness. He not only gave sight to this blind man but he also opened the eyes of his closest followers.

I'm convinced this story is not ultimately about Jesus' "inability" to heal a man on the first try. I believe it is a reminder that sometimes even those close to Jesus need another encounter with his life-changing power in order to see him clearly.

Is it possible that your vision of Jesus and his purpose for your life among the people closest to you is still blurry?

As you continue to grow in your relationship with Jesus, don't stop short of total restoration; seek the second touch of God.

Come to God today through prayer, and ask him to reveal the places where your vision of Jesus is still blurry. Ask him for a second, a third, or even a one-hundredth touch of healing. Allow God to restore your vision. There is no shame in asking God again and again!

GOING DEEPER

 Read: Mark 8:22–26

 Reflect

▸ In what ways is your vision of Jesus blurry?
▸ Where is your view of Jesus obscured by your disappointments or setbacks?
▸ Where do you struggle to see Jesus as he really is because of your cultural blind spots?

Pray

- Father, please show me where my vision of Jesus is still blurry.
- Father, please remove from my life any thing or any one obstructing my view of Jesus.
- Father, please open the eyes of my friends, family, and coworkers so they can see Jesus clearly.

Father, Please Help Me

REFLECT JESUS TO OTHERS

"'Come,' he replied, 'and you will see.' So they went and saw where he was staying, and they spent that day with him."
— John 1:39

HAVE YOU EVER been around someone who was so filled with the love and joy of God that you literally felt as though you were in the presence of Jesus himself? I remember meeting two such people—Dennis and Marsha Malone—several years ago during our church's Sunday night prayer service. I didn't know them at the time, but they stood out to me in the sea of faces that night. The median age in our church is still quite young, but during those years, it was even younger. Amidst the sea of college students and young adults stood these two senior saints who were more than twice the age of anyone else in the room.

But it wasn't their age that made them stand out the most; it was the way they worshipped Jesus that night with a level of unbridled joy unmatched by anyone else in the room that caught my attention. Their worship caused me to imagine what it must have been like to watch King David worship the Lord without hesitation as he danced with undignified abandon, much to the embarrassment of his wife (see 2 Sam. 6). I felt a sense of holy admiration and longing spread through the young adults who stood near Dennis and Marsha that evening.

We all got a glimpse of what it could look like to be madly in love with Jesus.

I'm so grateful that I went on to become close friends with Dennis and Marsha. After that night, they quickly became a treasured part of our church family as they started investing their time into the lives of young adults in our church family. They regularly opened up their lives to build friendships, pray with those who were struggling, and offer wisdom to those interested in faithfully following Jesus right here and now. Their encouragement was always rooted in Scripture, and their eyes glowed with the kindness of Jesus.

I always love running into a person right after they've spent considerable time with Dennis and Marsha. Without exception, anyone who is open to God's Spirit and has been in their presence comes away beaming with joy, hungry for the things of God.

I imagine this is what one of Jesus' earliest followers, Andrew, must have felt after returning from his first day of hanging out with Jesus (John 1:35–42).

After spending one day in the presence of Jesus, Andrew was convinced he had encountered the One for whom the people of God had been waiting. That's why he told his brother Simon Peter with great clarity, "We have found the Messiah!"

Have you ever wondered to yourself, *What in the world did Jesus say or do that day that gave Andrew such clarity about Jesus' identity as Messiah? Was it the way Jesus spoke? Was it Jesus' joy? Was it the way he interacted with others? Was it the way he listened attentively as people asked him one question after another? Was it a miracle Jesus performed?*

We don't know what convinced Andrew that Jesus was the Messiah; all we know is that hanging out with Jesus for one day opened his mind and changed his life forever.

The people with whom you interact on a daily basis need to hear the Good News of Jesus, without a doubt. But chances are that before they hear a sermon, they probably need to see one. Chances are they need to see the fruit of Jesus' life displayed in all of the ordinary moments of your life before they will truly listen.

My prayer is that you not only experience Jesus for yourself but you also grow in reflecting him well to others. I am convinced that Dennis and Marsha help others see Jesus so easily because they have so intimately and consistently *tasted and seen* the goodness of Jesus for themselves. Their public lives are merely the overflow of their personal friendship with Jesus.

How will you prioritize time with Jesus today? What would it look like to set aside a considerable amount of time for the sole purpose of building your friendship with him? The Bible promises that God draws near to us anytime we choose to draw near to him (Jam. 4:8). I encourage you to try it.

But don't keep the treasure of your time with God hidden from others. Ask God to help you be like Andrew (and my friends

Dennis and Marsha) today. Once you have experienced the goodness of God for yourself, ask God to show you whom you should share the joy of Jesus with today.

GOING DEEPER

 Read: John 1:35–42

 Reflect

▸ Who are the people God has used to help you see what the teachings of Jesus look like when they are lived out in our current cultural context?
▸ What would your non-Christian friends experience if they spent a normal day with you, your family, or your community of faith?

 Pray

▸ Father, give me a supernatural awareness of your presence today.
▸ Father, please show me how to make Jesus my first priority today.
▸ Father, please fill me with contagious joy so that others will come to believe that Jesus is the Son of God.
▸ Father, please help me to create space in my life for those around me so we can live in the daily adventure of following Jesus together.

Father, Please Help Me

NEVER BE TOO BUSY

"But *Jesus kept looking around to see who had done it*."
— Mark 5:30–32

ON A SUNNY afternoon during my sophomore year in college, I received a phone call from my dad while working at my part time job as an after-school counselor. I still remember where I was standing and the frenetic activity that was bustling around me as the kids played on the playground. I can still recall the sound of my dad's voice that day as he delivered the news that my mom had been diagnosed with stage 4 breast cancer.

For a moment, it seemed as though time stood still. The unexpected news had come so suddenly.

Shocked, I made my way into the main office, where my boss—a wonderful and godly woman named Mrs. Anderson—was knee-deep in managing the chaotic opening moments of the kids' after-school routine. Any other time, watching her help a group of nearly thirty elementary-aged children begin their homework, eat their snacks, and navigate their afternoon arts and crafts time was a thing of beauty. But today was different.

Without any consideration for the moment she was in, I blurted out,

> " My mom has cancer. "

I don't remember a single word she said, but what I do remember is the way she stopped what she was doing. She hugged me, looked deeply into my eyes, and treated me as though I was the only one in the room. Despite all of the pressing needs around her, she was not too busy to engage my pain.

One thing I love about Jesus is that *he's never too busy for our pain.*

Despite all of the demands of running the entire universe, he is always eager and willing to meet us in our great suffering.

I love the story of one such example from Mark 5. If the unfolding sequence were in a movie, the string of interruptions would be almost comical. But real-life stories recorded in Mark 5—of real people facing real challenges—feels heavy. In the story, Jesus' time among the crowds is interrupted by a frantic dad who has an extremely sick daughter on the verge of passing away. You don't have to be a parent to empathize with this father's sense of urgency. If someone you loved were about to die, you would be willing to barge into any public setting and make a scene if you thought it could make a difference.

At once, Jesus leaves what he is doing to help this terrified father. Yet on the way to help this man, a woman stops Jesus in his tracks. She had been bleeding for twelve years. Then, with the hope of healing in her heart, she reaches out to touch Jesus.

> Jesus' interruption was interrupted.

If ever there was a moment for someone like Jesus to just keep moving, this was it—a person was about to die! But luckily for us, Jesus thinks differently than we do. Somehow, he's never too busy for our pain. What a gift it is to have a God like him!

Today, you will likely encounter someone who is in a season of great pain. Their pain may be displayed on their chest for all to see, or it might be hidden. I wonder what it would look like if you asked God to open your eyes to the pain of those around you today. Even more, can you imagine what would happen if you asked God to use you as a source of hope and blessing to those around you who are hurting? I am convinced that God will honor prayers like that.

Read: Mark 5:21–43

 Reflect

▸ What has your experience of Jesus been like in seasons of pain?

▸ How can pain grow your faith or challenge it in seasons of grief or suffering?

▸ Whom do you know who is currently walking through a painful season? What is their name? What are they facing in particular?

▸ Are there any ways that Jesus is inviting you to tangibly care for them in the midst of their pain?

 Pray

▸ Father, please open my eyes to the pain of those around me.

▸ Father, please give me wisdom for when to share words of encouragement and when to be a quiet presence.

▸ Father, please help each person around me to see your goodness no matter their current situation.

DAY 19

Father, Please Help Me

LOVE THE BROKENHEARTED

"Blessed are those who mourn,
for *they will be comforted*."
— Matthew 5:4

EARLIER THIS YEAR, our next-door neighbor experienced the tragedy of losing her husband. It happened on a rainy Friday morning, completely unexpectedly. Although we all know death is inevitable (unless Jesus returns first), most of us live as though death will never come knocking on our door, so when it affects those we love, it nearly always feels too soon.

In the weeks and months following her husband's death, our sweet neighbor often told us how she felt like she was living in a fog. The moment of her husband's death changed everything. She suddenly found herself walking a path she never intended to travel.

As a follower of Jesus, she has great confidence in the promises of God, but for now, she is living in the pain of today.

If you have ever been in a place of deep pain like hers, you know this:

> It is difficult to live in between
> the pain and the promise.

I cannot imagine what the morning after Jesus' crucifixion must have felt like to Jesus' friends and followers: so much confusion, so much chaos—such deep grief. They had abandoned everything to follow Jesus—having left jobs, homes, friends, and even family—in the hope that Jesus was the One for whom they had all been waiting. And then, in a sudden turn of events, he was brutally killed.

Imagine their devastation.

Jesus' friends suddenly found themselves in the painful "in-between," and what made it worse was that many thought it was the end of the story altogether. They were living in between the shock of what had happened and the uncertainty of what was around the corner.

Their devastation led to deep mourning.

Perhaps they remembered Jesus' words about mourning from the sermon he had preached to them years earlier (recorded in Matthew 5:4). These words are so counterintuitive to our natural way of thinking that they feel nearly impossible to grasp or believe. He said, "Blessed are those who mourn . . ."

Really, Jesus? *Blessed?*

Honestly, I read those words and, from a human perspective, begin to wonder if Jesus knew what the word "blessed" even means. That's how upside down his teaching actually feels.

But he goes on to explain this counterintuitive proclamation: He says that the blessing is not the grief itself but the comfort that comes from God in the midst of grief. There is something about grief that opens up our ears and our hearts to the realness of God in a way that seasons of abundance rarely seem to produce.

Jesus reminds us what the psalmist so boldly declares in Psalm 34:18: that "God is near to the brokenhearted." From our perspective, there is nothing desirable about grief. Yet in the midst of the unwanted reality of suffering, God tends to show up in unimaginable ways.

How do you typically respond when you find yourself in a season of brokenness and pain? Are you in one right now? Is there someone around you who needs to experience the nearness of Jesus as they are swallowed up by a dark ocean of grief?

Is it possible that God is on the verge of turning this breakdown into a breakthrough? God has not abandoned you, and he has not abandoned those around you. He is near the brokenhearted. He comforts those who mourn.

Like Peter did when he was sinking in the water, may we call out to Jesus (Matt. 14:30).

As you pray today, ask God to meet you, and those around you, in your places of grief. Ask him to help you walk faithfully when the pain of Good Friday reverberates more loudly than the hope of Resurrection Sunday.

Read: Matthew 5:1–12

 Reflect

▸ Where do you need to receive the peace of God that goes beyond all understanding?

▸ Where do you need God to burn off the fog induced by grief with the warmth of his presence?

▸ Do you know anyone who is currently experiencing a season of extended mourning? How can you be a person of extended comfort?

 Pray

▸ Father, help me to be faithful to you in the painful seasons of my life.

▸ Father, help me to develop spiritual habits now that will carry me through these seasons.

▸ Father, help my friends and loved ones to walk closely with you in their places of grief.

▸ Father, please draw near to anyone around me who feels brokenhearted.

Father, Please Help Me

FOCUS ON ETERNITY

"When Jesus saw their faith, he said to the paralyzed man, '*Son, your sins are forgiven*.'"

— Mark 2:5

IN 2008, A twenty-four-year-old British man named Dante Knox decided to "sell his soul" on the popular auction site eBay. Fed up with the way his life was going, Dante started the bid for his soul at $32,000. The ad included a "buy it now" option for $896,000. Within a couple of hours, officials at eBay pulled the listing and released a statement saying:

> "You cannot sell anything that is not physical—that includes ghosts, souls, and spirits."[1]

For most people, this story was nothing more than a publicity stunt or humorous headline in the midst of the daily newsfeed,

---

1. Lesley Richardson, *Independent*, Dec. 15, 2008, https://www.independent.co.uk/life-style/gadgets-and-tech/news/dante-banned-from-selling-soul-on-ebay-1067893.html.

but for others it sparked an interesting debate around the value of a human soul. It certainly piqued my curiosity and caused me to reflect a bit.

Although the Internet might be ablaze with opinions regarding the worth of a human soul, the pages of Scripture are clear on this point: A soul is indescribably valuable in heaven's economy. The cross of Christ is heaven's bid on every human heart, and the truth is that our finite minds and hearts still cannot grasp just how significant that truth is.

One of my favorite stories from the early days of Jesus' earthly ministry, recorded in Mark 2, demonstrates Jesus' concern for a person's spiritual condition. At this point in his ministry, Jesus had become a burgeoning celebrity. Wherever he traveled, the crowds showed up en masse. On one such occasion, Jesus was staying with a friend when crowds of people showed up uninvited to get a glimpse of this man who was healing the sick and creating a stir wherever he went.

Jesus, in typical fashion, welcomed the uninvited throng of people and began teaching them the Word of God.

In the midst of this unplanned gathering, a group of guys, who were willing to do whatever was necessary to get their friend into the presence of Jesus, dug a hole through the roof and lowered their immobilized friend to the feet of Jesus.

Although the entire story is stunning and filled with deep truths, Jesus' initial words strike me the most. Mark tells us that when Jesus *saw their faith*, he was moved to bless this man. It's amazing to think how our compassion for others—like the compassion of this man's friends—coupled with faith in Jesus can pave the way for God to do great things in the lives of others.

But that's not the end of the story. I'm equally stunned by what happened next: After Jesus was moved by their faith, he turned to the man and forgave his sins.

Jesus certainly cared about this man's physical condition, but he was even more concerned with his spiritual condition.

The rest of the story clearly reveals how Jesus' response surprised everyone present. While he went on to heal the man's legs, it was the condition of the man's soul that captured Jesus' attention initially. Jesus' healing words prioritized the man's spiritual need above his physical needs. This way of thinking is so foreign to us as human beings, but I am convinced Jesus still moves in similar ways today.

> His healing power tends to
> work from the inside out.

As you pray today, I invite you to prayerfully read through this story from Mark 2 and let each part of the narrative sit with you. To whom do you most easily relate in the story? Are you one of the friends? Are you the man on the mat? Are you one of the skeptics in the crowd? Or are you a casual observer standing nearby?

As you pray through the story, ask Jesus to align you with his heart. Ask him to give you radical compassion for those caught in sin. Ask him to open the eyes of those around you to both the reality of their sin and his infinite capacity to forgive.

GOING DEEPER

 Read: Mark 2:1–11

 Reflect

- To whom do you relate the most in the story of Mark 2?
- When it comes to the needs of those around you, do you tend to notice their spiritual needs or their physical needs first?
- What are some practical ways you can help place your friends in the path of Jesus?

 Pray

- Father, please reveal any areas of sin in my life that disrupt my intimacy with you.
- Father, please give me your heart when it comes to the spiritual condition of those around me.
- Father, please give those around me a deep understanding of how much they need your forgiveness.

DAY 21

Father, Please Help Me

SEE WHERE YOU ARE WORKING

"But *blessed are your eyes
because they see . . .* "
— Matthew 13:16

MY FRIEND JANET has the uncanny ability to see the work of God everywhere. In fact, you cannot finish a conversation with Janet without her telling you about the ways she has recently seen the beauty of God's kingdom springing up all around. Her face lights up as she tells of how she witnessed God's creativity in the changing leaves of a red maple tree along the route of her morning commute.

Her laugh can fill a room as she describes how her second-grade Bible-class students are beginning to trust and follow Jesus. Her voice trembles with intensity as she recalls a powerful moment of worship, and she springs to life as she tells a story of getting to serve a person in need.

Janet sees the "bigness" of Jesus in the simplicity of everyday things.

She sees the kingdom of God everywhere.

Jesus began his earthly ministry with a simple yet awe-inducing invitation. As he looked out into a sea of listening faces—many of whom were experiencing great oppression at the hands of the Roman Empire—he declared a brand new way of life, open to any and all who would accept the invitation: "The *kingdom of God has come near*. Repent and believe the good news" (Mark 1:15).

Jesus joyfully declared that the kingdom of God was so close a person could reach out and touch it. But in order to experience it, they had to be able to see what God was doing right in front of them. No longer could they limit their understanding of the kingdom to the realm of religious endeavors.

> Jesus had not come to establish a religion;
> he came to unleash a mighty kingdom.

And yet, Jesus made it clear that unless we have the eyes to see it, we might just miss the work of God right in front of us.

There are times when we all need friends like Janet to help us see what God is doing right in front of us.

The invitation to see everything with "spiritual eyes" was foundational to Jesus' ministry. When Jesus sent his disciples ahead of him to spread the Good News in Luke 10, he began his pep talk by reminding them that God was already at work in the places they were getting ready to go. They just needed to keep their eyes open in order to see his activity.

I'm convinced that God is already powerfully at work in the lives of the people around you.

Do you believe that?

Can you see the beauty of the kingdom breaking in all around you? Are you able to recognize where God is already moving in people's lives at your workplace, in your neighborhood, or at your school? Do you long to partner with God in the ways he is already at work in the lives of those you love? He is eager for you to join with him in his kingdom!

As you pray today, ask God to give you his eyes, ears, and heart to participate in the kingdom of heaven right here and now. After all, the kingdom is so close you can touch it.

GOING DEEPER

 Read: Matthew 13:16–17

 Reflect

- ▶ Where do you see the kingdom of God at work around you?
- ▶ Where do you long to see the kingdom of God still break through?
- ▶ Where might God be inviting you to join him in the work he has already begun?

Pray

- ▸ Father, please give me the eyes to see and the ears to hear what Jesus is saying and doing in my life today.
- ▸ Father, please help me to see the world the way Jesus does with regard to every choice I make, big or small.
- ▸ Father, help me to live with a worldview that is shaped by the kingdom of light and not by the kingdom of darkness.
- ▸ Father, please help every person in my life to be born again by the power of your Spirit.

Father, Please Help Me

FAITHFULLY FOLLOW JESUS

"'Come, *follow me*,' Jesus said, 'and I will send you out to fish for people.' At once they left their nets and followed him."

Matthew 4:19–20

A FRIEND OF mine once served as an intern for a high-capacity politician who spent a lot of time in the public eye. My friend's job was pretty straightforward: Wherever his boss went, he followed. If his boss had an important dinner on a Tuesday night, he was there; if he had to speak to a group of dignitaries out of town, he was there; and if he needed someone to pick up his dry cleaning, he was the man for the job. His schedule was completely dependent on his boss's agenda. His daily activities were determined by the one to whom he reported.

Expectations were clear but not always easy. For example, I ran into my friend one morning after he had returned from a long stretch of serving in this new capacity. He made a statement that resonated with me deeply: He said, "I never realized, until now, how much I like being in charge of my own life and schedule."

Can you relate?

From a worldly perspective, maturity is often measured by a person's growth from *dependence to independence*. In fact, every coming-of-age story is typically built around a series of events found along the path to independence.

But from a spiritual perspective, maturity is measured in the opposite direction. It is measured as a person grows from independence to dependence. We are born with a deep longing to do things our way—just ask any mom with a two-year-old child. But by the grace and power of Jesus, over time, we learn to yield our will to the ways of Jesus.

If you want to experience the joy-filled life of God right here and right now, you must embrace the significance of two simple words: "Follow me." Not long after Jesus began his public ministry, he showed up at the workplace of a couple unsuspecting fishermen and gave them an invitation that would forever change their lives and begin to change the course of human history:

Follow me.

Jesus met these men where they were and invited them on a journey of discipleship.

The invitation for them was clear, but it was not always easy. In order for these men to experience the fullness of life with God, they had to totally abandon the notion that they were in charge of their life.

From this point forward, Jesus called the shots. He showed them where to go, what to do, when to sleep, and when to get up. He taught them what to say, think, feel, act, and do. He was now their leader; they were now his followers—not just his friends.

Jesus was clear from the beginning: Life in his kingdom is not an exercise in democracy. They don't get to vote or determine the direction of their kingdom activities. It is simply their job to follow.

If you don't personally know the goodness of Jesus, this invitation will likely seem absolutely absurd to you. Why would anyone hand over their ability to determine the course of their life? But when you come to know Jesus personally, the opportunity far outweighs the cost:

> Does following Jesus lead to uncertainties? Absolutely.
>
> Can following Jesus feel terrifying, confusing, and complex at times? Without a doubt.
>
> But the joy, peace, and freedom that come from walking in step with Jesus are far greater than anything we will have to surrender in order to follow him.

In the verse from Matthew 4 above, we read that upon receiving Jesus' invitation, the disciples left their nets "at once . . . and followed him."

That was their story. What's yours? Ask God to give you the courage today to follow Jesus wherever he might lead.

GOING DEEPER

 Read: Matthew 4:18–22

 Reflect

- ▶ In what areas of life do you still find it difficult to trust and follow Jesus?
- ▶ What joy and freedom have you experienced in the moments when you have learned to trust and follow Jesus?
- ▶ What does it look like on a practical level to follow Jesus in your daily routine?

 Pray

- ▶ Father, please reveal any ways in which I am still trying to get Jesus to *follow me*—my plans, dreams, desires, hopes, or wants—when he's called me to *follow him*.
- ▶ Father, help me to recognize the incomparable goodness of Jesus.
- ▶ Father, help my friends, family, neighbors, and coworkers to see the benefit of following Jesus.

Father, Please Help Me

JOYFULLY OBEY

"Simon answered, 'Master, we've worked hard
all night and haven't caught anything. But
because you say so, I will let down the nets.'"
— Luke 5:5

SEVERAL YEARS AGO while serving overseas, I had the privilege of sitting in a room with church leaders who serve in parts of the world where following Jesus is quite costly. To protect their safety, I will leave out the details of their personal stories, but allow me to share my experience with these amazing brothers and sisters:

For two hours, I listened in awe and through tears as they told story after story of what God was doing in some of the most dangerous places on earth for followers of Jesus:

> I listened to a woman tell the story of how her husband and children were murdered for their faith. Yet she went back to her village afterward and, with boldness and love, started a house church in the very village in which they had lost their lives.

> I met a former religious extremist and terrorist who was radically saved by Jesus and began sharing his faith with the very ones who were trying to exterminate Christianity in their part of the world.
>
> I heard a young man describe the incomprehensible joy of seeing a person who had once persecuted his family come to faith in Jesus—and become his brother in the faith.

With every story my faith grew, and my perspective and commitment to Jesus was challenged. Toward the end of the testimonies, we were given the opportunity to ask those in the room any questions we had. An older gentleman in the room asked a question that probably stirred in all of us: "In the face of such hardships, where do you find the courage to continue living so boldly?"

The young woman who had returned to plant a church in the village where her family had been killed was quick to respond. With tears streaming down her face and through a voice that was shaking, she gave an answer that struck a chord with everyone in the room:

> This is not about courage but about obedience. We are doing what we are doing because Jesus has asked us to do it.

As we venture to spend time with Jesus and do life with him, there will inevitably come moments when his instructions stand in conflict with our sense of reasoning.

I imagine that Simon Peter came face-to-face with this reality when Jesus stepped into his fishing boat and asked him to cast his nets for a second time. Jesus' instructions must have made absolutely no sense to Peter, given his long night's work with nothing to show for it and his professional expertise. Imagine what Simon probably thought when he heard Jesus' words:

> I'm a professional fisherman.
>
> I know what I am doing. Who are you?
>
> Jesus, you are a carpenter and a traveling preacher. What do you know about fishing?

This moment exposes the friction we often experience in our life with Jesus. Like Simon Peter, we all have to wrestle through the moments when Jesus' words stand in opposition to our understanding. We have to decide if we will be obedient, even when obeying Jesus contradicts our reasoning skills and capacity. What if his call on our lives is scary—or even dangerous?

During these moments we discover whether we are truly following Jesus or, instead, trying to get Jesus to follow us.

I love Simon's response in the face of a seemingly unusual request. To paraphrase, he says, "Jesus, I'm pretty good at fishing and I don't think your instructions make much sense, but because you say so, I will do this."

As you enter another day of prayer, ask God to transform you into a "because you say so" kind of person. Ask him to transform you into a person who is eager to joyfully obey Jesus no matter the cost. I wonder what God might choose to do in and through you if you wholeheartedly embrace this posture.

Read: Luke 5:1–11

 Reflect

▸ Have you ever had a moment when Jesus' words were in conflict with your understanding of how life is supposed to work?
▸ Why do you think Simon Peter was able to trust Jesus beyond the borders of his understanding?
▸ Are there any places in your life where you are refusing to surrender your will to Jesus' words?

 Pray

▸ Father, please help me to obey you, even when your instructions don't make sense to me.
▸ Father, please help me to become a "because you say so" kind of person.
▸ Father, please show me the places in my life where I have allowed my human understanding to deter my obedience to you.
▸ Father, please help those around me to experience the power of your presence in a way they cannot ignore.

Father, Please Help Me

BE A FRIEND TO SINNERS

"Jesus . . . looked up and said to him, 'Zacchaeus, come down immediately. *I must stay at your house today*.' So he came down at once and welcomed him gladly."

— Luke 19:5–6

WHILE I WAS in seminary, I became friends with a man who, from an academic perspective, was not a star student but from a practical, put-your-faith-into-practice perspective was running laps around most of us in the class. He loved Jesus and he loved all sorts of different people too. Most of his friends were rough around the edges. Most of them were not church-going, Bible-believing, well-mannered folks. In fact, many people didn't know what to do with him because of the company he kept around him.

Many in our class were suspicious of his "commitment to the faith" because of the people he hung out with and the places he frequented. This suspicion always perplexed him (and for good reason) because, after all, we were in graduate school to supposedly learn how to become more like the One who was often called a "friend of sinners" (Matt. 11:19)

> Religious people didn't know what to
> do with Jesus or his rowdy friends.

They still don't.

Back in the day, people were constantly trying to label Jesus. His admirers did so out of respect; his critics did so out of disdain. But no label was sufficient to encompass the fullness of Jesus. One of my favorite labels of Jesus, "a friend of sinners," actually came from the mouths of his critics.

With this label, they attempted to dishonor Jesus. But it actually portrayed—and still portrays now—the beauty of Jesus' heart with more truth and clarity than they could possibly understand at the time.

In Luke 19, Jesus put his heart for sinners on display through his friendship with one of the most despicable sinners of the day, a tax collector named Zacchaeus. Not only was this man viewed as a traitor working to oppress the people but he was also getting rich while doing it! By virtue of his job alone, Zacchaeus was a hated man.

But Jesus didn't hate him. In fact, Zacchaeus was the object of Jesus' affection.

He was the reason Jesus had come in the first place.

I love the scene of Jesus walking through Zacchaeus's town: The crowds pressed into the crowded streets like Times Square on New Year's Eve. In the midst of all the noise, joy, congestion, confusion, and chaos, Jesus looked up to see this hated sinner who was actually trying to get a glimpse of him. Jesus always had an eye for the desperate.

Can you imagine everyone's surprise—especially Zacchaeus's—when Jesus not only knew his name but also wanted to spend time with him! Jesus declared, "Come down immediately. I must stay at your house today" (Luke 19:5). Put yourself in Zacchaeus's shoes for a moment. Imagine what it felt like to discover that Jesus (the most loved man in the region) was eager to hang with you (the most despised person in town).

This is the heart of Jesus, and his heart is the same for all sinners today: His heart overflows with <u>love</u> not just toward Zacchaeus but also toward you and me—and toward every human being, regardless of their sin record.

Jesus knows who you are, and he knows what you have done—both the good and the bad. He has come to town, called you by name, and wants to take up residence in your heart. But this is true not just for you; it is true for those around you as well.

As you pray today, ask God to help you develop meaningful friendships with people who feel as though they are spiritual outsiders.

Read: Luke 19:1–10

 Reflect

- How do your friends resemble or differ from Jesus' friends?
- Do you know any spiritual nomads who are beginning to grow curious with regard to Jesus?
- What characteristics in a person might help you to identify someone as a spiritually curious person?

 Pray

- Father, help me to recognize that I am a sinner in need of your grace, just like Zacchaeus.
- Father, please grow my curiosity for Jesus today.
- Father, please help those around me who are stuck in sin to see clearly that Jesus really is a friend of sinners.

DAY 25

Father, Please Help Me

SEARCH FOR THE MISSING

"Suppose one of you has a hundred sheep and loses one of them. Doesn't he leave the ninety-nine in the open country and *go after the lost sheep until he finds it*?"

— Luke 15:4

YEARS AGO, MY friend's son went missing. Although the story had a happy ending, several hours were marked by great fear and uncertainty while the story unfolded. During the time he was missing, those who knew of the situation cleared their schedules, cancelled lunch meetings, and skipped appointments until my friend's son was home, safe and sound.

In that moment, I experienced something I had always assumed to be true but hadn't come to know first-hand until then. I learned this:

When a child goes missing, normal people go looking.

I can relate to my friend because not long ago I too lost one of my sons for a very short but terrifying stretch of time. Time stood still and worry flooded my mind. Losing a child is a parent's worst nightmare. I cannot imagine what courses through the heart of our heavenly Father as he continuously witnesses the wayward choices of his beloved kids. I don't know how he handles it.

There is lot of research and data currently being discussed, dissected, and disseminated in Christian circles with regard to the religious decline in the American church. Although the data is quite helpful, I am concerned that the language we often use to describe the religious habits of Americans desensitizes our hearts to the reality of what is happening. The primary problem is not that people are reprioritizing their weekend habits (although that too matters); the main problem is this: Many of God's beloved children have gone missing.

In Luke 15, Jesus tells a series of stories about the ways God's children go missing from the family of God. Although there are many ways to be lost—wandering like a sheep, getting dropped like a coin, running away like a rebellious son, or pouting like an older brother who didn't get his way—there is one consistent response from our heavenly Father: compassionate pursuit.

Our Father's pursuit comes in all shapes and sizes.

Sometimes he pursues wandering sheep like a good shepherd—leaving the ninety-nine and traversing the backcountry to rescue even just one sheep caught in the thicket—and he finds us when we have been ensnared by sin and false beliefs, places us on his shoulders, and carries us home.

Other times he searches for us like a woman who has lost a valuable treasure: He gently removes everything from the house, shines a light into every dark corner of our past, and when he finds us, he gently dusts us off and holds us close.

And then there are the times when he waits for us like a patient father—he stands on the porch until we come to our senses. He knows that unless we come face-to-face with sin's empty promises, we will keep being lured away to that distant country of destitution. Then, the moment we turn back, he comes running toward us, eager to restore.

Yet still other times, he pursues us like a father pleading with his disgruntled and self-righteous son, sharing his heart, and gently inviting us back into the party.

There are many ways humanity gets lost, but thankfully God is better at seeking than we are at hiding.

Do you know someone who's "gone missing"? Have you had any friends go missing from the family of God in recent years simply because they got distracted and wandered off? Have you had any friends who have been dropped or wounded, perhaps by their religious experiences? Have you had anyone in your life run from the Father's house in rebellion? Have you had anyone you know shut themselves off to God because of their pride or self-righteousness?

Perhaps you find yourself in one of these situations. Perhaps you woke up recently to discover that you aren't where you want to be spiritually. I know that's happened to me—and it's not fun—but there's hope for us all.

As you seek God in prayer today, ask him to use you to bring one of his missing children home. Can you imagine what would happen if every*one* found some*one*? I'm convinced those who have been found take great joy in finding other people, which is good news because God wants to use us in someone else's redemption story!

GOING DEEPER

 Read: Luke 15

 Reflect

▶ Do you know anyone who has wandered from God?
▶ Can you identify any emotional, relational, intellectual, or physical barriers that would make it challenging for them to "return home to God"?
▶ How do you sense God might be positioning you to play a part in their redemption story?

 Pray

▶ Father, please help me to notice those who have wandered from your family.
▶ Father, please give me wisdom on how to partner with Jesus and bring them home.
▶ Father, please help each of my lost neighbors, coworkers, family members, and friends to turn away from any choices that are keeping them from turning to you.

DAY 26

Father, Please Help Me

SHOW AND TELL

"*Heal the sick* who are there *and tell them,*
'The kingdom of God has come near to you.'"
— Luke 10:9

WHEN MY BOYS were young, they always looked forward to Friday because Friday meant show and tell at school. Each week, the kids were allowed to bring a favorite toy or item from home to share with the class. There was only one rule for the game: Before you could tell the class about your toy, you had to show the class how it worked.

Simple, right? You had to *show them* before you could *tell them*.

In Luke 10, Jesus sent his disciples out into the nearby villages to deliver the Good News that the kingdom of God had come near—and he gave them very specific instructions. He said, to paraphrase, "Before you tell them that the kingdom is here, I want you to show them what the kingdom actually looks like" (10:9).

I believe the order here is important: Although life in the king-dom often requires us to "believe it before we see it," Jesus knew that for many people their first step into the kingdom would come as they caught a glimpse of heaven on earth.

> Most people need to see a
> sermon before they hear one.

There are some amazing servant-leaders in our region who take this show-and-tell reality to heart. Several nights a week they hit the streets to serve the poorest of the poor in Nashville. They provide meals, free haircuts, and free showers, not to mention helping the poor with small medical needs, job training, and transportation assistance. They even help former prisoners find employment and addicts begin the long, slow journey to freedom.

Not only do they provide incredible physical services but they also do it all in the context of gospel friendship. They meet the needs of those who are suffering in a way that allows them to see the kingdom of God so that when they hear about it, it makes sense.

As many of the people they serve begin to grow curious about the love they are seeing and receiving, this team of servant-lead-ers shares the story of Jesus with them in ways they can begin to apply to their everyday life.

Jesus modeled and taught that the kingdom of God is some-thing that needs to be both *seen and heard.*

In our current religious climate, there is a tendency for people to pit these two realities of word and action against each other. Some people believe our mission is simply to show the world what the love of Jesus looks like, while others believe the emphasis should be on sharing the Good News primarily with words.

In Jesus' kingdom, words and works are never at odds; they are complementary. How is Jesus inviting you to display the goodness of his kingdom to those around you today? Where is he inviting you to demonstrate its beauty through service to others or through prayers of supernatural breakthrough in the life of someone around you?

Or maybe you have been demonstrating the kingdom faithfully, and now Jesus is inviting you to declare it. Where is Jesus inviting you to tell someone that the God of love is closer than they might currently perceive?

As you pray today, ask God to help you grow in your ability to show others and tell others about the goodness of Jesus.

GOING DEEPER

 Read: Luke 10:1–24

 Reflect

▶ Do you find it easier to show or tell others about the goodness of Jesus?

- ▶ Why do you think you tend to lean in that direction?
- ▶ Are there any practical steps you sense Jesus inviting you to take toward showing or telling about the kingdom among the people you love?

 ### *Pray*

- ▶ Father, please help me to be a show-and-tell kind of person.
- ▶ Father, give me the power to demonstrate the kingdom with boldness and beauty to those around me.
- ▶ Father, please help me to declare the kingdom with grace and clarity to those around me.

Father, Please Help Me

LEVERAGE MY PASSION

"Come, follow me . . . and I will send
you out to fish for people."
— Mark 1:17

I BELIEVE THAT it brings God great joy when we discover
the ways our passions can be leveraged for his purposes.

I have been so inspired by people who have found creative ways
to use their talents to point to God's goodness:

> Ben uses soccer to build relationships with kids in under-
> served neighborhoods.
>
> Cynthia uses her leadership gifts to create safe and
> healthy work environments for employees who have been
> neglected or abused.
>
> Helga uses art to introduce people to the goodness of
> Jesus.

Randy uses his dentistry to care for refugees who have just moved to the States.

Clint and Dan use their boat to connect with and serve young kids who are in need of mentorship.

Mary uses her nursing skills to care for and bless people in challenging times.

Trey uses his woodworking skills to help men in recovery occupy their mind and body with a new hobby.

Jamie uses music to tell redemptive stories.

DJ uses real estate as an open door to care for families at key transitions in life.

God is using these people to fulfill his purposes—and he wants to use your passions to do the same.

I don't think it's a coincidence that Jesus told a group of fishermen that he was going to teach them *how to fish for people.* Although Jesus was certainly using the metaphor of fishing to help them understand a kingdom reality, I have often wondered if Jesus was being more literal than we tend to think.

It would be interesting to know how many men and women from the little fishing communities where these fishermen lived came to trust and follow Jesus through conversations that were had as they fished alongside his first disciples.

> In my experience, Jesus loves to use people's passions to reveal his glory.

I love the story in Matthew 17 when Peter is approached by the local tax collector and reminded that he owes taxes. Considering Peter had already quit his job to follow Jesus, this must have made Peter quite nervous. But Jesus wasn't worried. Do you remember what he sent Peter to do? He sent him fishing—again. Peter followed Jesus' instructions, once again, and came back with a good story to tell, not to mention coins to pay their taxes.

Although this story reveals a variety of beautiful truths, I love what it reveals with regard to Jesus' ability to use our talents for his purposes. Jesus sent Peter back to do the thing he knew all too well—fishing—and through that Jesus revealed his power in a fresh way once again.

What do you know how to do? What are you good at? What do you love to do? I wonder how God might be trying to unleash your gifts and passions for his purposes in the world? How might you use your gifts and passions to bless the people you encounter on a regular basis, in the places you live, work, and play?

How might you use your hobby to create a place of community for those who need godly friendship? How could you use your unique skillsets to bless a person in need? How could you use a special skill to serve your church family? I believe the love of God is often channeled most clearly through us when we allow him to receive glory through the things we love.

As you pray today, ask God to open your eyes to practical ways your gifts and passions can be used for his glory and for the good of someone else today.

Read: Matthew 17:24–27

 Reflect

▸ How have you experienced the goodness of God through the way someone else used their gift or passion to bless you?

▸ What gifts and passions has God given you that could be used to bless someone else?

▸ What is a simple way you could use something you love to point others to Jesus?

 Pray

▸ Father, please help me to use all of my life for all of your glory.

▸ Father, please give me simple opportunities to use what I love to bless others in Jesus' name.

▸ Father, please help those near me to experience your goodness in a very real way today.

Father, Please Help Me

HAVE THE COURAGE TO GO

"He told them, *'The harvest is plentiful, but the workers are few . . . Go! I am sending you out* like lambs among wolves.'"
— Luke 10:2–3

I RECENTLY ATTENDED a meeting with several hundred missionaries from all over the world. It was quite the experience. An older man in the room spoke and reflected back on what was one of the most painful memories in his lifetime of serving with global missions. He told a story from nearly three decades earlier, when a large number of missionaries had gathered together to prayerfully develop a plan for reaching all of the "unreached and unengaged" people groups in the world. (If you are unfamiliar with this term, it simply refers to a group of people who have not yet heard the Good News of Jesus.)

The older man spoke of how the group had joyfully gathered because they were committed to finishing the work that Jesus called his followers to take seriously in Matthew 28:16–20. They wanted to see disciples made in every nation.

But the joy in the room soon became sorrow once it was clear that there were certain places in the world to which no one in the room was willing to go.

Ultimately the mission convention ended with a period of awkward silence and frustration as those present realized the greatest challenge was not a lack of opportunity but ultimately a lack of willingness to go.

As he was telling that story, I found myself both frustrated and sad. I thought to myself, *How could that be?* But then, the Holy Spirit began showing me the many places in our own city and beyond that I am unwilling to go.

The late Oswald J. Smith once made a haunting statement that has challenged me for years:

> "
> Why should anyone hear the gospel twice when some people have still not heard it once?
> "

A shortage of spiritual opportunity is never the issue in the eyes of Jesus. No, as he reminds us, "The harvest is plentiful, but the workers are few. Ask the Lord of the harvest, therefore, to send out workers into his harvest field" (Luke 10:2).

The spiritual opportunities are abundant, but what about our willingness to go?

Can you imagine what would happen if you simply asked Jesus to send you to any place—near or far—that was ready for spiritual harvest?

Would you be interested in taking on that assignment? Imagine the joy you would experience as God used your willingness to shape the eternal destiny of other human beings.

Perhaps you have questions, but what would happen if we simply removed the fine print and went wherever Jesus sent us? What would change if we came to Jesus without conditions? I challenge you to go to God with open hands and ask Jesus to increase the number of spiritual workers today by starting with you and those around you.

As you pray today, ask God not only to raise up more workers for the spiritual harvest but also ask Jesus to raise up others to journey with you as well (from your church, neighborhood, school, place of work, etc.).

GOING DEEPER

 Read: Luke 10:1–24

 Reflect

▸ Are you currently living as one who has been "sent by Jesus" into the places where you already live, work, and play?

▸ Have you asked Jesus recently if there is any place to which or any people to whom he is sending you for his purposes?

- How many faithful followers of Jesus do you think it would take to serve and care for the needs of the people around you where you live, work, and play?

 ### *Pray*

- Father, please send me into the harvest field.
- Father, please use me to show the world just how wonderful you are, whether in my own neighborhood or among the nations.
- Father, please give me courage to simply say yes as you call me to go on mission with you.
- Father, please help every person I encounter on a regular basis to find a meaningful, truth-seeking, and Spirit-filled local church to call home.

Father, Please Help Me

LEAN ON YOUR PRESENCE

"... and surely *I am with you always,*
to the very end of the age."
— Matthew 28:20

A FRIEND OF mine has a beautiful yet intense calling of ministering to people in their final days of life. Ecclesiastes 7:2 tells us that it is "better to go to the house of mourning than to the house of feasting." In other words, people tend to have a deeper sensitivity to the things that matter most as they approach the end of life, as opposed to during seasons of great strength and prosperity.

My friend knows this well.

In fact, she recently told me a story about a woman to whom she had been ministering for weeks. This sweet woman had spent most of her life—including her final days—greatly resisting the reality of Jesus and his love for her.

Day after day my friend would enter her room, serve her, listen to her, care for her, and quietly pray for her. Yet this older woman remained obstinate.

Throughout her season of caring for this woman, my friend would often ask a small group of us to pray for spiritual breakthrough in the woman's heart. One day, I asked my friend how it was going, and she made a comment that struck a chord in my soul and reminded me of Jesus' words in Matthew 28:20 (quoted above). She said,

> I don't know how Jesus is going to do it, but I know that he is in the room with us. He is going to show me how to help her see his goodness.

In other words, she wasn't worried because she knew the end results weren't up to her. She simply needed to report for duty and trust that Jesus was present with her in the process.

If you desire to make Jesus' words from Matthew 28 quoted above—to make disciples wherever you go—your life's first priority, then he promises to be intricately involved with you in that process. It doesn't matter if you are a school teacher, an accountant, a musician, a business owner, a student, a stay-at-home parent, or someone in between jobs.

This is true for all of us:

Jesus promises to be actively present when we align our lives around his priorities.

Imagine with me how freeing it would be if you truly believed that Jesus is present with you every time you stop to talk with your neighbor. Can you imagine how empowered you would feel in the breakroom at work if you truly believed that the Son of God was with you as you navigated that tricky conversation with your coworkers? What would happen if you could see Jesus sitting with you as you hung out with your fraternity brothers or sorority sisters? How would his literal presence around your Thanksgiving dinner table transform the way you talk about faith with your relatives who don't yet trust and follow Jesus?

Jesus isn't just *for you*; he is also *with you.* His Spirit lives in you!

Let the promise of his presence be your source of peace today as you prayerfully seek to make Jesus known wherever you go.

GOING DEEPER

 Read: John 14–16

 Reflect

▸ How would your confidence increase when it comes to sharing your faith if you truly believed that Jesus was not just *for you* but also *with you*?

▸ Can you remember a moment when the Holy Spirit guided you as you ministered to someone in need?

Pray

- ▸ Father, please fill me with more of your Holy Spirit so I can help others see Jesus today.
- ▸ Father, help me to live with a continual awareness of your presence with me.
- ▸ Father, please give those around me an increased hunger for your presence.

Father, Please Help Me

BECOME MORE LIKE JESUS

"You will conceive and give birth to a son,
and you are to call him Jesus. He will be great
and will be called the Son of the Most High."
— Luke 1:31–32

WE BEGAN THIS journey of prayer thirty days ago with one simple question: How would life improve for the people around you if Jesus was their neighbor? This wasn't just about your actual neighbors but also about anyone around you that you encounter in your daily life.

As we come to the end of our month-long journey of prayer, I'm reminded of a recent lunch conversation. One of my friends at lunch that day was nearly six months pregnant. She looked at the men sitting around our table and said, "I sure do wish you guys could feel what it is like to have human being growing inside of you!"

We all began to laugh, and all of us guys readily admitted how grateful we were to experience that reality only as spectators. I have known some pretty tough guys over the years, but I have yet to meet any guy who thought he was tough enough to carry and give birth to a baby.

I vividly recall many of the conversations my wife, Sydney, and I had as she was pregnant with each of our sons. Week by week we would talk about the size of the little life actively growing inside of her as we followed the pregnancy charts. Sydney would say things like, "Right now, he is the size of a bean," or, "Soon, he will be the size of a lime." Other times, we would find ourselves in tears as we heard our son's heartbeat for the first time, or excited as we felt him actively kicking inside of Sydney's stomach.

> It is a beautiful and sacred mystery to watch *a life grow within another life.*

Can you imagine how Mary must have felt when she discovered that she had been entrusted to carry the Son of God in her womb? She must have been overwhelmed with joy and fear as she began to process both the privilege and the responsibility of carrying Jesus, the Son of God, inside her body. I wonder what it would have felt like to know that day by day the divine was growing inside of her. Try to imagine that for a moment.

Although our *physical* assignments are different than Mary's, our *spiritual* assignments are the same. In Galatians 4:19, the apostle Paul reminds us that the goal of the Christian life is that the fullness of Jesus be formed in us. In other words, for every follower of Jesus, the presence of Christ should be growing to maturity within us day by day, from the second we are saved until the moment we see Jesus face-to-face!

What would it look like for Jesus to be more fully formed in you?

What parts of your life would begin to change if you let Jesus grow more fully in your life?

What would it look like for his thoughts to become your thoughts, his ways to become your ways, and his love to become your love?

The truth is that Jesus has indeed moved into your neighborhood. Not only did he come into the world more than 2,000 years ago but he also continues to move by his Spirit into any place where he is joyfully invited. Every time Jesus inhabits a human heart, he begins to change that person—from the inside out. As this transformation happens over time in each one of us, those around us will see less of us and more of Jesus being formed in us.

By the love of the Father, the grace of the Son, and the power of the Holy Spirit, we begin to see those around us as Jesus sees them. As we begin to love them as Jesus loves them, we will more easily offer our hearts, hands, mouth, feet, and whatever else we have to give to love them well. We will begin to serve them as Jesus serves them.

No longer will those around us merely experience *us*; they will begin to experience *Christ in us*!

As you come to the end of this thirty-day journey of prayer, take some time to thank God for the ways you have witnessed

Jesus being formed in you. Also, set aside some space to ask God where he is still working to form Jesus more fully in you.

In addition, take some time to reflect on how you have seen Jesus at work in the lives of those around you this month. Did any of the people you were praying for experience a place of spiritual breakthrough in their relationship with Jesus? Did anyone on your prayer list take a step forward in their journey of faith?

Finally, take a moment to dwell on the treasure of Christ living in you by the power of his Spirit. What a gift! How exactly will this divine gift continue to bless those around you in the days, weeks, months, and years to come? Only God knows the answer, but we can trust that it will be great!

GOING DEEPER

 Read: Galatians 5

 Reflect

- ▶ Where are you beginning to see Jesus' life more fully formed in you?
- ▶ Do you sense any places where you might be resisting God's formative work in you?
- ▶ How would life begin to improve for those around you if you embraced this truth of Christ in you with more intentionality on a daily basis?

Pray

▶ Father, please help me to grow in awareness of both the privilege and the responsibility of Jesus living within me.
▶ Father, please grow Jesus' heart, mind, and love within me.
▶ Father, please keep growing my passion for you and those around me beyond this thirty-day prayer experience.
▶ Father, please reveal yourself to my friends and family members who don't yet know you.

A PRAYER FOR STAYING THE COURSE

"Let us not become weary in doing good, for at the proper time we will reap a harvest *if we do not give up.*"
— Galatians 6:9

I hope the last thirty days of prayer was life-changing for you:

> *I hope each day was filled with joy and deep intimacy, as you made time to talk with God.*

> *I hope you experienced the thrill of following Jesus in new ways, as you spent time praying for the people around you with new levels of intentionality.*

> *I hope you saw God open doors for meaningful relationships and conversations around what matters most.*

> *I hope you feel more strength and clarity with regard to Jesus' purpose for you in your current season of life.*

But maybe the last month didn't go the way you had hoped.

> *Maybe praying for others didn't come naturally.*

> *Maybe you didn't see many open doors in the lives of the people for whom you were praying.*

> *Or maybe you never really got into a good rhythm and you are a bit discouraged about your lack of spiritual discipline.*

It's okay. I've been there myself—many times.

Whether the last month was life-changing or disappointing, I'm convinced God has more in store for you if you will keep taking small steps toward him and toward others.

I want to end this journey with a simple prayer. Feel free to pray this prayer with me or pray it in your own words:

> *Father, thank you for the way you love us. We come to you and we ask that you would help us to stay the course. Please don't let us grow tired of doing good. Thank you for all that you have done over the course of the last month—the things we have seen and the things we have yet to see come to pass. Thank you for the way you have been at work in both the struggles and in the successes. Father, as we finish this particular part of our journey, help us to continue with a fresh commitment to keep praying for and serving the people you have put all around us. Father, help us to persevere in prayer. Father increase our de-*

sire to be with you, and give us the discipline to go along with it. Father, help us to invest in the lives of those you've put around us—for the long haul. Father, use our lives to make an eternal difference.

In the name of Jesus, amen.

About the Author

DAVE CLAYTON is a follower of Jesus, a husband to Sydney, and a dad to Micah, Jack, and Judah. He lives in Nashville, Tennessee, where he has the joy of serving Ethos Church, Onward Church Planting, and Awaken Nashville. Dave is passionate about making disciples, planting churches, and awakening a movement for the glory of God, the joy of the church, and the good of the multitudes who don't yet know Jesus.